Walt Disney World®
20 Magical Years

This book is dedicated to

He had the courage and vision
to follow his dream.

Without Walt's inspiration and drive,
Walt Disney World would never have been conceived,
much less built.
Although he was only one man,
he touched the lives of countless millions.
He refreshed our spirits
by appealing to the child in all of us.
Each time he turned one of his dreams into reality,
he showed us that our own dreams can come true.

"Somehow I can't believe there are many heights
that can't be scaled by a man who knows
the secret of making dreams come true."
Walt Disney

Contents

GRAND
FLORIDIAN

TYPHOON
LAGOON

Introduction

Walt Disney was a man who always lived on the edge of tomorrow. His dreams seemed impossible to others, but he dared to make them come true.

We know him, first, as a filmmaking pioneer. The first synchronized sound cartoon, *Steamboat Willie* (1928) was his creation, as was the first full-color cartoon, *Flowers and Trees* (1932). He was also responsible for the first animated film that gave the illusion of depth through the use of the multiplane camera, *The Old Mill* (1937).

The cartoon, as realized by Disney, gained even greater stature in 1937 when Walt released his first full-length animated feature, *Snow White and the Seven Dwarfs.* He went on to introduce many more innovations to moviemaking, including stereophonic sound (*Fantasia,* 1940) and 360-degree projection (Disneyland's Circle-Vision 360, 1955).

Walt Disney was a man of many milestones. Among them were: Mickey Mouse, surely the most popular cartoon character ever created, and Snow White and the Seven Dwarfs, *called "Disney's folly" before it was released, but nonetheless a financial and artistic success.*

Other milestones in Walt Disney's life were: "Walt Disney's Wonderful World of Color" (far left), America's longest-running prime time television program (its title changed over the years); the development of Audio-Animatronics *for shows like "The Enchanted Tiki Room" (left); and a unique theme park called Disneyland (shown below at its dedication.)*

This remarkable man's many achievements also include the longest-running prime time television series (1954-1983), the Academy Award-winning True-Life Adventure nature films, which revolutionized the documentary genre, and the development of true three-dimensional animation through the electronic wizardry of the *Audio-Animatronics* system.

But Walt Disney's dream that had perhaps the most far-reaching effect on life in America was the one about a "magical little park." He called it Disneyland. It was one of the most important entertainment landmarks of the twentieth century.

When Disneyland opened on July 17, 1955, in Anaheim, California, it was the realization of a 20-year-old dream for Walt, its chief "imagineer."

First rendering of Disneyland sketched in 1953.

"The idea came along," Walt said, "when I was taking my daughters around to those kiddy parks. While they were on the merry-go-round, riding 40 times or something, I'd be sitting there trying to figure out what I could do." Those often unsatisfying afternoons gave him the notion of a family park that would be as entertaining for adults as for children.

"It took many years," Walt said. "I started with many ideas, threw them away, and started all over again." Eventually, Walt's "family park" became Disneyland.

Not an amusement park, and certainly not a kiddyland, Disneyland was like nothing the world had ever experienced. Walt had developed the concepts for the Park on his own, with little consideration for what the world thought an amusement park should be.

He used the ideas and skills of his filmmakers to create a giant outdoor stage, with sets dressed for comedy, drama, and adventure. On each set, everything from architecture, landscaping, and costumes to food, music, and sound effects was orchestrated down to the smallest detail, creating a totally themed environment.

And Walt saw his guests not as spectators, but as participants in the performance. All the intricate elements of his theme-park "show" would have been wasted, if the guests hadn't been there to play their parts.

As we all know, Disneyland was an overwhelming success. Less than two years after it opened, it had become, in the words of *Time* magazine, "America's biggest tourist attraction."

Walt announced his plans for a themed resort in Florida (left). On the site near Orlando (below), he reviews plans with, from left, his brother, Roy O. Disney, former Disney Productions Chairman Card Walker and Admiral Joe Fowler, who supervised the construction of Walt Disney World. More than 8,000 workers, representing every kind of building skill, worked on the construction of the Vacation Kingdom. At the peak of construction in 1970, this was the largest private construction project in the United States.

But Walt Disney was never one to rest on his laurels. Even as Disneyland was enjoying unprecedented success, he was preparing to "imagineer" his greatest dream—Walt Disney World.

One of the things Walt realized after Disneyland was built was that he should have bought a much bigger parcel of land. Speculators had snapped up the surrounding property and cluttered the environs of the Magic Kingdom with fast-food establishments and motels. For Walt, this detracted from the magical experience that he felt Disneyland should be.

So when the land was acquired in Florida for Walt Disney World, it amounted to over 150 times the acreage of Disneyland—27,500 acres, to be exact. On the property, Walt envisioned another Magic Kingdom, but also hotel and recreational facilities that would provide a complete vacation opportunity for the whole family.

Walt Disney died in 1966, shortly after introducing his concepts for the Florida project. But the organization he had built, led by his brother Roy, plunged ahead with the development of the first phase of Walt Disney World—the vacation resort. The painstaking imagineering process continued for five years, transforming paintings, scale models, and blueprints into a three-dimensional, full-sized realization of one of Walt's fondest dreams.

In the photo above, a Disney Imagineer programs the movements of an Audio-Animatronics parrot, a cast member in Pirates of the Caribbean. An engineer (right) compares a scale model of the submarine, Nautilus, *to the first full-size replica to be built. A craftsman (center left) applies genuine gold leaf to the statue ruins for the under-sea voyage of the* Nautilus, *and two workmen (lower left) install a friendly hippo in the Jungle Cruise. Below is a photo of one of the costume workrooms that keep the entire cast looking great.*

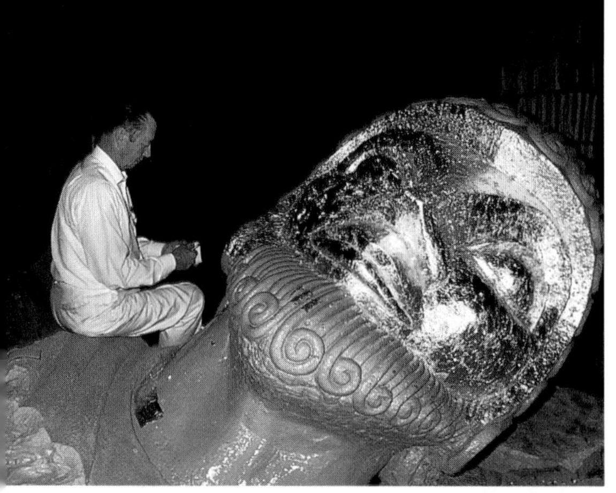

More than eight million cubic yards of earth were moved in the construction of the first phase of Walt Disney World. Meticulous care was lavished on even the smallest detail, so that guests would really feel as if they were in another world. The submarines for 20,000 Leagues Under the Sea (bottom right) were built in Tampa and then transported to Walt Disney World, where they now sail a mysterious underwater world.

A Disney Imagineer programs Henry, the host of the Country Bear Jamboree, while an artist puts the final paint details on the tiger that lives in the temple ruins of the Jungle Cruise (seen under construction to the right.) The Haunted Mansion (below) rises from the banks of the Rivers of America.

The Building of a Fairytale Castle

The landmark around which all of the Magic Kingdom is built is Cinderella Castle. Here is how this internationally known landmark went from designers' visions to reality. Cinderella Castle is said to be the most photographed man-made structure in history.

At the same time The Magic Kingdom was rising from the ground, the hotels and other resort areas were also being constructed. Disney's Contemporary Resort Hotel (left) rises on the banks of Bay Lake. Disney's Polynesian Village nestles quietly beside the Seven Seas Lagoon, and Pioneer Hall (bottom), home of the "Hoop-Dee-Doo Musical Revue," is built at Disney's Fort Wilderness Campground.

On October 1, 1971, the Walt Disney World Vacation Kingdom opened to an eager public. One year and nearly 11 million guests later, it had already become one of the top-ranking vacation spots in the world, attracting more people in a year than the United Kingdom, Austria or Germany.

Walt Disney World's opening celebration lasted throughout the month of October, 1971. Its highlights were a gala concert by the 60-nation World Symphony Orchestra under the direction of Arthur Fiedler; a spectacular luau at Disney's Polynesian Village Resort; the dedication of Disney's Contemporary Resort Hotel by comedian Bob Hope; and the Magic Kingdom's opening parade, featuring a 1,076-piece marching band directed by composer Meredith Willson. Taking part in the televised opening festivities were Julie Andrews, Glen Campbell, Buddy Hackett, Jonathan Winters and a "who's who" of American entertainment, business, government, and industry.

Walt Disney's brother and partner for 40 years, Roy O. Disney, and Walt's very special friend, Mickey Mouse (above), dedicated Walt Disney World. In a message delivered to the Walt Disney World cast on the eve of opening day, Roy wrote:

"Years of planning and long hours of work have brought about this historic moment. It will be an experience none of us will forget.

"At this time, I think it is appropriate that we remember Walt's comment: 'You can dream, design, and build the most wonderful place in the world, but it requires people to make the dream a reality.'

"You, the cast, are responsible for making Walt's dream come true . . . yesterday, today, and tomorrow."

By EPCOT Center's opening day in 1982, nearly 3,000 designers, 1,000 consultants, and 10,000 construction workers had participated in its creation. Some 54 million cubic feet of earth were moved and 20,000 tons of steel erected. Over half a million board feet of lumber had become 2,000 show props and sets. And the Walt Disney World Monorail network was extended 7.5 miles to include EPCOT Center.

When Walt Disney came to Florida, he was looking far beyond his lifetime to the creation of an entire Experimental Prototype Community of Tomorrow.

In fact, as early as 1964, Walt had begun to develop concepts for EPCOT Center. This is how he described his great idea:

EPCOT will take its cue from the new ideas and new technologies that are now emerging from the creative centers of tomorrow that will never be completed, but will always be introducing and testing and demonstrating new materials and systems. And EPCOT will be a showcase to the world for the ingenuity and imagination of American free enterprise.

The Disney organization had creative resources unique in corporate America. It had a permanent staff of designers, engineers, artists, writers, architects, electronics and computer specialists, and many other talented people with dozens of craft and professional skills. Together they brought to life Walt Disney's greatest dream.

EPCOT Center is a breathtaking voyage into the world of the future, and an international journey through the nations of the world. It is the world of the possible: In Future World, the challenges of life in the next century are vividly explored.

EPCOT Center is also the world of today and yesterday: In World Showcase, the cultures and achievements of different nations are presented in all their colorful diversity.

Wherever we look in EPCOT Center, we see Walt's vision made real. The achievements of the past and present are integrated with the wonders of the future.

Future World blends creative showmanship with dazzling new technologies to create the look of tomorrow. Its uniquely designed pavilions and exhibit areas provide close-up explorations of communications, energy, life in the 21st century, transportation, imagination, agriculture, and the ocean. Each pavilion of Future World explores the past, present, and future of its complex subject matter through presentations that range from drama to whimsy.

If Future World's look of tomorrow is the heart of EPCOT Center, World Showcase, with its kaleidoscope of international experiences, is its soul. A community of nations in miniature, World Showcase focuses on the cultures, traditions and accomplishments of people from around the globe. It is the only permanent exposition of its kind anywhere.

Walt Disney believed that people could develop a solution to any problem, if they had the right information, technology, and opportunity.

Together, Future World and World Showcase offer a new look at what our world can be, through understanding, cooperation, and a better knowledge of each other. As Walt intended, EPCOT Center is an endeavor by people, for people, with hope for a better world.

A sky full of multicolored balloons, hundreds of trained pigeons trailing red and blue streamers and fluttering white doves signaled the opening of EPCOT Center on October 1, 1982. Rooftop trumpeters heralded the elaborate ceremonies, while a Goodyear blimp cruised overhead.

Disney Chairman Card Walker gave the dedication, hailing the combination of Future World and World Showcase as an "enormous tribute to American ingenuity."

In 1986 the Walt Disney Company began construction of its third theme park and the first fully functional movie studio in Florida: the Disney-MGM Studios Theme Park. The park required the talents of thousands of designers, artisans, craftsmen, and construction specialists. It took more than three years to build the opening phase of the Disney-MGM Studios.

Aerial view (top) shows the Disney-MGM Studios Theme Park under full construction. A giant Mickey Mouse is given a lift up to his place of honor high atop the Crossroads of the World (left). Below is a closer look at Lakeside Circle under construction.

A studio landmark, the "Earffel Tower," (above) is fitted with its own mouse ears. Disney Imagineers (right) evaluate one of the many site models prepared before construction. A Disney craftsman (below) installs part of the Temple set for the Great Movie Ride and an artist finishes a Disney version of an Egyptian wall hieroglyph. (Bottom) Imagineers examine C3PO, the host of Star Tours in the Backlot annex.

The Magic Kingdom

The Magic Kingdom

It would be difficult to find better words to describe this very special place than "The Magic Kingdom." It is a world apart from the real, where a magical kaleidoscope of yesterday, today and tomorrow touches the hearts and minds of young and old alike. Here the sense of wonder that is often buried beneath the weight of everyday problems can bubble up into fun and laughter.

Come with us now—forget your cares. Stroll through a memory, and set sail on a dream for tomorrow.

THE MAGIC KINGDOM
WALT DISNEY WORLD

Main Street, U.S.A.

The first of the Magic Kingdom's six themed "lands," Main Street, U.S.A. is a nostalgic tour of an enduring symbol of American life—a turn-of-the-century small town. Main Street gives us a tantalizing look at the best of the "good old days." It is America between 1890 and 1910, when a burgeoning technology was replacing real horsepower with mechanical horsepower, and the telephone, telegraph, phonograph, radio and cheap, available hydroelectric power were revolutionizing daily life. The style was curlicues and gingerbread. Every town, no matter how small, had its imposing city hall, usually fronted by a spacious plaza with a bandstand.

Step with us into this exciting era of contrasts. Welcome to Main Street, U.S.A.!

You can find many kinds of old-time vehicles up and down Main Street. The horseless carriages, double-decker buses, bright red fire engine and horse-drawn trolleys of the Main Street Transportation company cruise from the Plaza to Cinderella Castle and back again. The Belgian and Percheron draft horses who pull the trolleys weigh close to a ton each, and are shod with plastic rather than steel, because that's easier on their hooves. They work two or three hours a day, three or four days a week, and when they're not working, they doze and munch sweet green hay at their barn in Fort Wilderness.

Main Street is a wonderful place to shop. You can buy clocks, silk flowers, party decorations, magic tricks and monster masks. You can also purchase fine porcelain, hand-blown glassware and all kinds of Disney merchandise. Main Street is also a place to eat. Wonderful meals may be had at the Town Square Cafe and the Plaza Restaurant. Snack on a pastry from the Main Street Baker, a cool ice cream cone from the Ice Cream Parlor, or some crunchy popcorn from one of the bright red popcorn wagons.

Six classic Mickey Mouse cartoons from the 1920's and 30's, including Mickey's first film, Steamboat Willie, *flicker across the movie screens of the Main Street Cinema.*

The "Walter E. Disney," "Lilly Belle," "Roger E. Broggie" and "Roy O. Disney" are steam engines of the Walt Disney World Railroad. Originally built between 1915 and 1928, they hauled jute, sugar, hemp and passengers throughout the southern jungles of Mexico. After being purchased from United Railways of Yucatan, they were disassembled and shipped to the Gulf Coast for complete renovation. Now each engine pulls five open-sided passenger cars, departing from the Main Street Railroad Station for a one-and-a-half-mile tour around the Magic Kingdom.

(Top right) The City Hall Information Center provides information and assistance on entertainment, reservations, transportation and lost and found.

The Dapper Dans (top left) ride a bicycle built for four, but they also sing barbershop melodies and do a mean soft-shoe. Rainbows of blooms decorate the flower market, while balloon vendors can be found up and down Main Street. The Crystal Palace restaurant is a place to dine in old-fashioned Victorian splendor, surrounded by white wickerwork and tall palm trees. The sun-filled atrium reminds you of the elegant British conservatories that were popular in the 1800s.

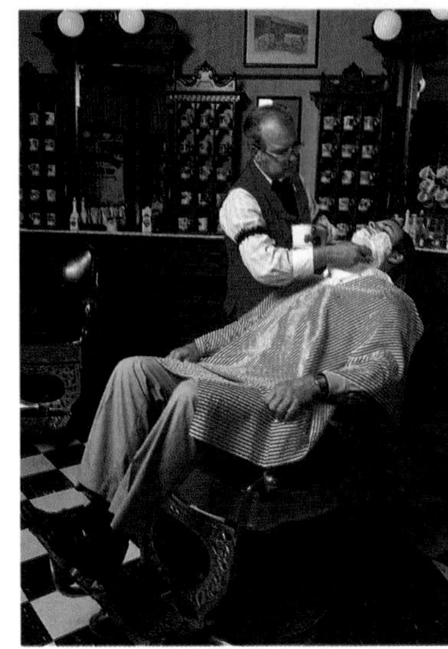

Main Street at night is a panorama of light, from small, twinkling flashes to wide, steady glows. The firehouse of Engine Company 71 (The Magic Kingdom opened in 1971) is aglow with Victorian architectural detail. The Penny Arcade has an old-time collection of authentic games, like a Kiss-O-Meter, a coin-operated antique band organ, tests of strength, and some very early "moving pictures."

Fantasyland

Reaching gracefully up to Florida's intense blue sky at the end of Main Street is Cinderella Castle, the entrance to the Magic Kingdom's most fanciful realm.

This enchanting 180-foot-high landmark is an architectural blend of many European styles, from 13th-century French fortress to late Renaissance palace. Since it was inspired by no single structure, Cinderella Castle represents all castles. It is the solid yet dream-like setting for countless childhood fantasies.

In the castle courtyard stands a charming bronze statue of Cinderella, heroine of the fairytale that inspired the 1950 Disney animated classic film.

Artistry and craftsmanship also find expression inside Cinderella Castle, where five mosaic panels depicting scenes from the Perrault fairy tale adorn the foyer walls. Each of these wondrous murals is 15 feet high and ten feet wide. They were fashioned out of more than 500 colors of jewel-like Italian glass, in millions of bits, some of them as small as the head of a tack. Genuine sterling silver and 14-karat gold have also been used in the mosaics, which tell the story of the gentle scullery maid who became a princess.

These glittering murals would dazzle even a fairy godmother, but they are only a sample of the castle's infinite detail. The Disney family crest is carved above the castle's Gothic entrance. In King Stefan's Banquet Hall hang hand-stitched medieval banners, and finely detailed gargoyles peer from their lofty perches atop the castle's spiraling towers. All in all, this landmark is a true visual feast.

From the Skyway to Tomorrowland, which departs from a Swiss chalet near Peter Pan's Flight, you can look down on the colorful pageant of Fantasyland. Here you might have asked Alice and the White Rabbit why they're so late, soared high into the sky with Dumbo the flying elephant, or watched as Wendy tucked her brother Michael into bed, telling him stories of Peter Pan. This boy who wouldn't grow up lived in a whimsical realm called Never Land, where, with his tribe of Lost Boys, he pow-wowed with Indians and fought pirates.

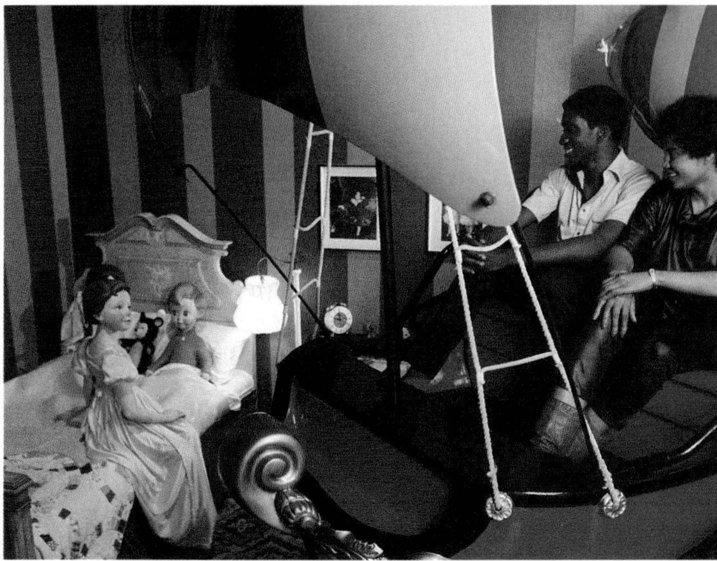

Beyond the castle drawbridge is the land that Walt Disney called "a timeless land of entertainment." This is Fantasyland, dedicated to all those children, young and old, who believe that dreams really can come true.

Here you can fly high with Dumbo or whirl in a spinning tea cup, take a gallop on a mighty white merry-go-round steed, or careen with Mr. Toad down the road to Nowhere in Particular. You can refuse the poison apple in the outstretched hand of the Wicked Witch or duck as Captain Hook fires his cannon. Here Disney fantasies are yours to enjoy.

In 1963, the people at Pepsi-Cola asked Walt Disney to create a pavilion for the 1964-65 New York World's Fair. It's a Small World was an immediate hit. And since the time it made its permanent home in Fantasyland, this salute to the children of the world has consistently been one of the Magic Kingdom's favorite entertainments. Dozens of artists, model makers, engineers, musicians, sculptors, architects, costume designers, lighting experts and other artisans used their skills to create a unique international voyage. It's a Small World proves that it really *is* a small world, after all.

Created by some of the world's most skilled woodcarvers in 1917, Cinderella's Golden Carrousel (left) was in disrepair when found by Disney scouts at a park in Maplewood, New Jersey during the 1960s. It measures 60 feet in diameter, and is one of the largest carrousels ever built. Beneath thick layers of paint covering the horses, artisans discovered elaborate detail surviving in gleaming wood.

Disney designers replaced a few stationary chariots on the carrousel with additional galloping horses, raising the number of steeds from 72 to 90. Each horse has its own unique decoration, but all the horses are white, so that everyone has the chance to ride a white horse.

Inspired by the crazy Unbirthday Party in Alice in Wonderland, the Mad Tea Party teacups (above) give guests a dizzying ride! Then it's off on a whirling flight on Dumbo, the Flying Elephant (below). Created in honor of Mickey Mouse's 60th birthday celebration, Mickey's Starland (left) captures all the whimsy of vintage Disney cartoons. Here's where Mouseketeers of all ages have a chance to meet Mickey and his pals.

The inspiration for Fantasyland, of course, was provided by Disney's classic animated films, namely *Snow White and the Seven Dwarfs*, 1937 (Snow White's Scary Adventures); *Pinocchio*, 1940 (Pinocchio's Village Haus snack bar); *Dumbo*, 1941 (Dumbo the Flying Elephant); *The Adventures of Ichabod and Mr. Toad*, 1949 (Mr. Toad's Wild Ride); *Cinderella*, 1950 (Cinderella Castle and Cinderella's Golden Carrousel); *Alice in Wonderland*, 1951 (Mad Tea Party and The Mad Hatter hat shop); *Peter Pan*, 1953 (Peter Pan's Flight and Tinker Bell Toy Shop); *Sleeping Beauty*, 1959 (King Stefan's Banquet Hall restaurant); *The Sword in the Stone*, 1963 (Merlin's Magic Shop); *The Aristocats*, 1970 (The AristoCats gift shop); and *The Black Cauldron*, 1985 (Gurgi's Munchies and Crunchies Snack Bar).

The bug-eyed sea serpent below is actually one of 12 submarines that take you 20,000 Leagues Under the Sea. Each vessel carries 38 passengers into a mysterious underwater world inspired by Walt Disney's 1954 Academy Award-winning film based on Jules Verne's science-fiction classic. As you cruise through the eerie blue-green world, you might even sight human divers among the Audio-Animatronics treasure hunters.

One outstanding live-action film also inspired an attraction in Fantasyland. In 20,000 Leagues Under the Sea, sea monster-like submarines chart an eerie voyage to Vulcania, Captain Nemo's South Seas hideaway. Slipping silently into a peaceful tropical lagoon, the submarines take us through coral reefs and sunless caverns, even beneath the Arctic ice.

This breathtaking underwater world is actually made of steel, fiberglass, stucco, epoxy paint and gold leaf. They transform an 11.5 million-gallon tank into a watery wonderland of icebergs, rock formations, sea grass, kelp, giant clams, seahorses and corals of every shape and hue.

Adventureland

Exotic trees and bushes, vines and flowers were brought from the world's tropical regions to Florida's mild climate for Adventureland, which is the most lushly planted of all the Magic Kingdom's six realms. Among the varied species are Cape honeysuckle from South Africa, Canary Island date palms and Mexican flame vines.

When creating Adventureland, Disney Imagineers strove to make it "a wonderland of Nature's own design." And it is obvious to anyone who journeys through this exotic land that this direction was followed, leaf, stalk and petal.

A veritable United Nations of plants was assembled to represent the tropic regions of the world. From the South Pacific to the West Indies, from darkest Africa to the densest Amazon, flowering trees and shrubs radiate the spectrum in brilliant, ever-changing patterns of blossoms. Vigorously twining vines and vast stands of bamboo, palms, ferns and grasses add contrasting textures and cooling shades of green.

Adventureland's architecture and decoration, too, are typical of tropical climes—palm-thatched roofs, South Sea idols, cool shuttered rooms and lazy ceiling fans. The rattan patterns and wrought-iron traceries call to mind the colonial empires of Britain and Spain.

Shops in Adventureland offer merchandise from Hong Kong, Thailand, Africa, India and the islands of the Caribbean. Polynesian entrees as well as hamburgers are served at the Adventureland Veranda, while the Sunshine Tree Terrace serves cooling fruit juices.

Two of the Magic Kingdom's most popular attractions are to be found in Adventureland. One is the Jungle Cruise; the other is Pirates of the Caribbean. The latter is situated in Caribbean Plaza, a Spanish-style enclave of pastel stucco walls and red tile roofs. Here meandering walkways, hidden courtyards, tile-lined fountains and colorful flowers grace an outdoor bazaar as picturesque as any ever found on the Spanish Main.

The Jungle Cruise takes you through a Southeast Asian jungle, the Nile Valley, the African plains and the rain forest of the Amazon River. Along the way, you meet yawning hippopotami, playful bathing elephants, a sinister slithering python and a group of fearsome headhunters.

One of the most unusual Magic Kingdom experiences is the Jungle Cruise, which sends you off down tropical rivers in a gaily-striped launch. Your guide has a decidedly offbeat sense of humor, which runs to remarks like "Keep your hands and arms inside the boat! Those crocodiles are looking for a handout."

The Jungle Cruise is a favorite of armchair explorers, because it compresses weeks of safari travel into ten minutes of fun, without mosquitos, monsoons or misadventures.

Adventureland's Caribbean Plaza is where you find one of the Magic Kingdom's most popular attractions – Pirates of the Caribbean. The story line is about a disaster – the capture, pillaging and burning of a seacoast town by a crew of swashbucklers who would shiver the timbers of Blackbeard. Yet, scurrilous as they are, there is something distinctly un-menacing about these rapscallion rogues. And while their victims may fret just a bit, they seem to be having as much fun as the buccaneers.

One special tree in Adventureland is a creation of steel and concrete, not a natural phenomenon. The Swiss Family Treehouse, inspired by a 1960 Disney film, is built in a unique Disneyodendron eximius *("extraordinary Disney tree"). It weighs over 200 tons, and its concrete roots go 42 feet deep into the Florida soil. Its 90-foot crown is covered with 800,000 vinyl leaves on 600 spreading branches.*

Two hundred twenty-five singing birds, crooning flowers and chanting tiki gods fill the Sunshine Pavilion with the happy sounds of Tropical Serenade. When the musical-comedy revue reaches its peak, the celebration is suddenly halted by a violent thunderstorm unleashed by angered island gods. But the unflappable masters of ceremonies, José, Michael, Pierre and Fritz, carry on in time-honored show business tradition.

Frontierland

Walt Disney had a special respect for the men and women who pushed America's western boundary to the Pacific Ocean. Frontierland is his tribute to those hardy pioneers. Its landscape blends towering conifer forests of the Pacific Northwest, red-and-ochre-hued deserts of the Southwest and Mississippi river landings. Its frontier way of life is symbolized by the coonskin cap and the cowboy hat, the calico sunbonnet and the plantation straw.

Frontierland is set in a timespan of some eighty years, from 1790 to 1870. It recalls some of the most colorful aspects of American history. Here are the boisterous frontier of Davy Crockett and the rollicking dance hall of an Old West town, the elegant life-style of the Old South and the eerie loneliness of an abandoned ghost town. Here, too, are the comforting safety of a cavalry stockade and the hard-scrabble days of the Gold Rush.

Frontierland is built along a waterway called the Rivers of America. As you glide along its shore, you can see Big Thunder Mountain, Fort Sam Clemens, Tom Sawyer Island and Grizzly Hall. You will also pass a colorful Indian village, a burning settler's cabin and wildlife like moose and deer.

One of the highlights of a visit to Frontierland is the Diamond Horseshoe Jamboree, a half-hour-long show that tickles everyone's fancy, from the simplest to the most sophisticated. Its talented performers consist of Miss Lily Langtree, a glamorous chanteuse, a trio of saucy, charming can-can dancers, Sam the bartender, who is also owner, boss, chief cook and bottlewasher at the Diamond Horseshoe Saloon, and his three handsome, athletic cowboy assistants.

A highlight in the hijinks occurs when Sam asks two volunteers from the audience to help him with the sound effects for a truly indescribable rendition of the old children's favorite, "Old MacDonald."

Frontierland's atmosphere is one of old, weathered western towns, whose buildings were unpainted and sometimes leaned against one another. Authentic frontier touches are provided by old kerosene lanterns, wooden kegs and barrels, many kinds of cactus and denim-garbed hosts and hostesses. Sidewalks are the raised wooden kind that were meant to keep skirts and boots out of the mud and dust. The river landings look like they must have in the days when the Mississippi River was considered the wild West.

Ten years of planning and 18 months of construction went into Big Thunder Mountain, not to mention 630 tons of steel, 4,675 tons of specially-formulated "mud," and more than 9,000 gallons of paint. At $17 million, Big Thunder's cost equaled that of Disneyland at its 1955 opening. More than $300,000 was spent on authentic set decorations alone. So convincing are the rusty hues of weathered and eroded rock in the mountain that an observer could easily be fooled into thinking he's looking at natural elements that have been weathering in the Florida wind and sun for thousands of years.

Big Thunder Mountain's weathered buttes tower 197 feet above ground, making this two-acre landmark the highest "mountain" in Florida. Its runaway mine trains whisk you into yawning caverns, past bubbling phosphorescent pools and steaming volcanic lakes, beneath raging waterfalls, through an earthquake and a flash flood. The partially buried and sunbleached bones of an ancient dinosaur complete the impression that you really have just taken the "wildest ride in the wilderness."

Three kinds of craft ply the Rivers of America—shallow-draft keelboats, a Mississippi stern wheeler and primitive log rafts.

The Mike Fink Keelboats commemorate an old-time riverman who lived from 1770 to 1823, and who knew Davy Crockett. The *Gullywhumper* and the *Bertha Mae* are designed for shallow-water navigation.

The *Richard F. Irvine* is named for one of the chief designers of Disneyland and Walt Disney World. It is an authentic, steampowered reproduction of the great white "river queens."

The log rafts, of course, are modeled after the one on which Tom Sawyer and Huckleberry Finn set out on many of their adventures along the wide Mississippi River.

Tom Sawyer Island is a youngster's dream. No sidewalks here—just grass-edged footpaths. Situated in a loop of the Rivers of America, this primitive playground has Harper's Mill, a creaky waterwheel with a working windmill and a dark, scary cave where you just might meet Injun Joe. There are two bridges on the island. One is an old-fashioned suspension bridge that swings. The other is a barrel bridge, which floats on air-tight steel drums. This latter is lots of fun for the kids, because when one person bounces on it, everyone has to bounce.

Cross the barrel bridge and you find yourself at Fort Sam Clemens, named for Tom Sawyer's creator, who wrote under the pen name, Mark Twain. This fort is a rugged, backwoods stockade. In the guardhouse is a comical bum and his snoring dog, and on the second floor of the fort is an old-fashioned shooting gallery, where make-believe soldiers can improve their marksmanship.

BIG
AL
TRAIL
BEAR

At Grizzly Hall, the lifelike *Audio-Animatronics* cast includes 17 bears, a raccoon and talking buffalo, stag and moose heads. They put on one of the funniest shows in the Magic Kingdom, the Country Bear Jamboree. This theatrical production has a little bit of Bluegrass in the Five Bear Rugs and Liver Lips McGrowl, a little bit of Western in the Sun Bonnets, Bunny, Bubbles and Beulah, and a little bit of Dance Hall in Teddi Barra's knockout performance on a flowered swing.

It's an unbearably funny show, and relies on precisely timed comedy and music. The Country Bear Jamboree makes you react to the bears as if they were real, as you clap, sing along, and shout for encores.

In Country Bear Jamboree, the Five Bear Rugs and the Sun Bonnets, accompanied by Gomer on the piano, play and sing at center stage (top). The show also features thousands of pounds of animated "Bearitones," including Big Al (left), whose antics nearly stop the show. Also featured is Teddi Barra (above), a glamorous songstress who descends dramatically on a flower-decked swing.

Liberty Square

Step onto Liberty Square and you'll walk back across the pages of American history to the Eve of Independence—1776. Here life in the Thirteen Colonies and the Spirit of '76 have been reborn.

In contrast to Frontierland, the atmosphere in Liberty Square recalls the early American cities and seacoast. The blend of colonial architecture includes the Dutch New Amsterdam designs found along the Hudson River, as well as the Georgian style of Williamsburg, Virginia, and the Federal style of Philadelphia. Along the waterfront the buildings assume a New England character.

To sample colonial hospitality, guests may visit the Liberty Tree Tavern or Columbia Harbour House. For a taste of patriotic spirit, there is a great "publick" meeting hall, echoing the colonists' challenge to "tyrannie."

Liberty Square is also the site of two very popular attractions, The Hall of Presidents and The Haunted Mansion.

The Liberty Tree Tavern captures the warmth and hospitality of a colonial inn from the 18th century. Its windows are fashioned from handmade "seed glass," and each of its six dining areas features a unique fireplace. The Columbia Harbor House (right) offers New England seafood cuisine, as well as traditional colonial chicken and turkey dishes.

Antique crystal decanters, colonial china and early American furniture can be found at Olde World Antiques. At Mlle. Lafayette's Parfumerie, you may have a fragrance blended just for you. Each personal scent is assigned an identification number so that it can be reordered by mail. The Silversmith shop offers sterling and pewter gifts like those in vogue during the 1700s.

The original Liberty Tree was christened in Boston in 1765, when the Sons of Liberty gathered beneath its boughs to protest the imposition of the Stamp Act. The Liberty Oak Tree in the Magic Kingdom is a hundred-year-old southern live oak, quercus virginiana. *Found six miles from its present home in Liberty Square, it is about 40 feet tall and 60 feet wide, and weighs more than 38 tons. It is by far the largest living specimen in the Magic Kingdom, and probably one of the largest ever transplanted. It was lifted out of its original site by using steel rods inserted through the hardwood center of the trunk. The transplant required not only skill and patience, but a good deal of "knock on wood" luck. Today, the Liberty Oak Tree looks as though it had been growing happily in Liberty Square since the Revolution.*

While the Liberty Oak Tree commemorates the militant spirit of the American Revolution, the great colonial hall in Liberty Square was designed to recall the Boston and Philadelphia meeting houses in which the young republic's two most important documents – the Declaration of Independence and the Constitution – were forged. Its red brick walls look as fresh and new as they must have in the days when Thomas Jefferson, George Washington and others gathered to create a new nation. The date above its door – 1787 – is the date that the Constitution of the United States was ratified.

In his role as spokesman for all the Presidents, Abraham Lincoln delivers a stirring patriotic address. "All the armies of Europe, Asia and Africa combined," he says, "could not by force take a drink from the Ohio, or make a track on the Blue Ridge."

More than 15 years of work went into The Hall of Presidents before its debut. Sculptors alone spent two years creating the life-size figures of presidents Washington (below) through Nixon for Opening Day in 1971. Presidents Ford, Carter, Reagan and Bush were added as they took office.

The Hall of Presidents, whose steeple dominates the Liberty Square skyline, is reminiscent of the famous assembly houses found in several eastern capitals. The stately building also showcases one of the most exciting applications of the *Audio-Animatronics* system, which has been employed to portray the importance of the American heritage and the vitality of the United States Constitution. The production, entitled "One Nation Under God," leaves no guest unmoved.

A highlight of the presentation is seeing all 40 Presidents of the United States together on one enormous stage, in life-size and lifelike form. As the roll call begins, each Chief Executive, from George Washington to George Bush, acknowledges the announcement of his name.

Then Abraham Lincoln rises to speak for all the Presidents. The words of his powerful oratory, assembled from six of his speeches, prove as inspirational today as they were when spoken more than a century ago. And as this 16th President speaks, his colleagues react to his stirring message with nods and gestures. The overall effect is entrancing. Although you know that the 40 figures aren't real, it's easy to react to them as if they were living men.

Not far from the Hall of Presidents is a residence designed to scare up some early American fantasy and folklore. High on a bluff overlooking the Rivers of America, the stone-faced Haunted Mansion presents the ominous spectre of a Dutch manor house from the Hudson River Valley. It's an architectural style perhaps best described as early Edgar Allan Poe.

On nights when the moon is a ghostly galleon and the sky is a cloudy sea, one might well imagine Ichabod Crane riding this way on his fateful journey through Sleepy Hollow.

A giant bat hovers above the dagger-shaped belfry. Inside the Haunted Mansion, an unbroken chain of "doom buggies" carries guests through chambers and halls equipped with wall-to-wall screams and cold-running chills.

The mansion offers a happy haunting ground and *very* active retirement for 999 ghosts, ghouls and goblins, who are just dying to take you on a frightfully funny adventure.

The Haunted Mansion's happy haunts include ghostly dancers twirling to an eerie waltz, a spectral organist who sits at a cobweb-draped pipe organ, a creepy king whose crown is tipsy, and a mournful bride whose heart still beats true for her long-lost love. Eerie apparitions invade endless hallways. There's rapping on a door, but no one is there, and a piano is played by unseen hands, while the pianist's shadow bleeds across the floor.

The Haunted Mansion may be a poltergeist's paradise, but for Disney maintenance crews, it's a veritable nightmare. To keep it nice and dirty, furnishings must constantly be covered with dust, and corners with cobwebs.

"Dust" is purchased by the pound and distributed like grass seed from hand spreaders. Yet it seems to evaporate into thin air. Legend has it that since the Magic Kingdom opened in 1971, maintenance personnel have spread enough dust to *bury* the Haunted Mansion.

Tomorrowland

As you pass under Tomorrowland's entry pylons, you enter the one Magic Kingdom realm whose theme is the future. Its clean, simple architecture speaks to us of a time when technology has taken over many of life's tedious tasks, leaving us free to pursue intellectual and artistic goals. Even the landscaping complements this impression, as does the serene waterway surrounding this land.

Adventures on the move, around the globe and out among the stars, that's Tomorrowland. Among the experiences you can enjoy are a revolutionary transportation system called the WEDway PeopleMover, a thrilling race through the cosmos in Space Mountain or a realistic Mission to Mars.

Simply by definition, Tomorrowland poses one of the Magic Kingdom's greatest challenges to designers. Because the future is a moving target, Tomorrowland must undergo continual updating.

Stimulating sensations of space flight are experienced inside Space Mountain. Ten years in development, the gleaming white cone-shaped mountain is an engineering marvel. It's big enough to cover a football field, and its intricate track system was designed with the aid of computers. And because the rocket guideways are virtually invisible, you experience a sort of unanchored acceleration that seems to lift you beyond the pull of gravity.

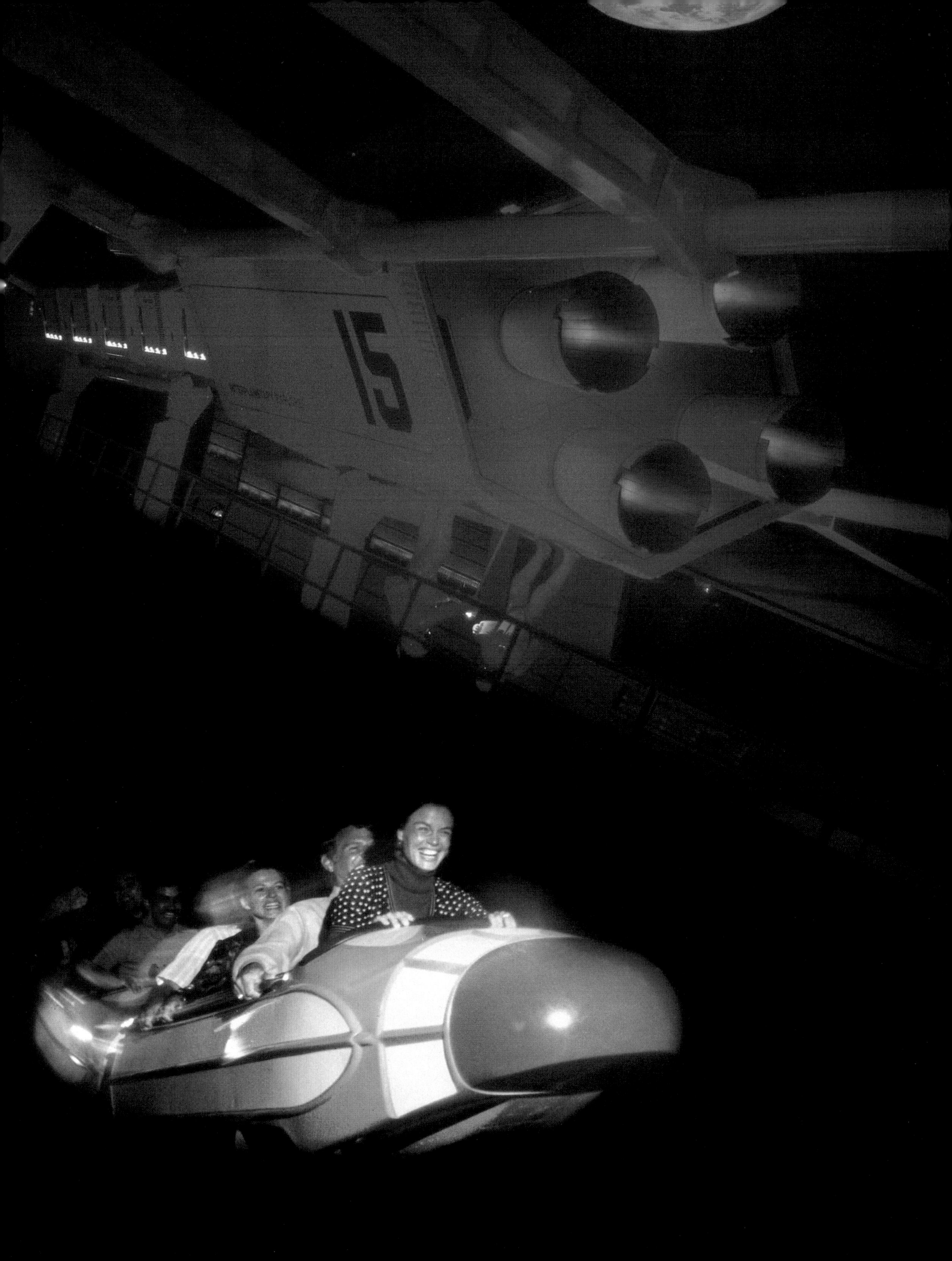
15

When you board the Disney-engineered WEDway PeopleMover, you board a state-of-the-art transportation system. Its elevated track saves the land from being carved into a roadbed, and spares the air from pollution, because it relies on electrical power. Except for the sliding doors and wheels, WEDway vehicles have no moving parts. With few parts to wear out, there are virtually no maintenance costs. The WEDway system is different from other "people mover" systems in that the drive power is in the track, not in the vehicles. This unique form of transportation made its debut in a commercial use when it was installed at Houston International Airport in 1981.

Of course, one person's thrills are another's chills. The thrill rides are not for everyone. Happily, Tomorrowland offers other unique excursions.

Aboard Carousel of Progress, the stage stays put and the audience revolves to see a lively *Audio-Animatronics* review that traces electricity's growing role in the American home.

In the Circle-Vision 360 Theater, "American Journeys" literally surrounds us with the sights and sounds of a tour of the United States. A Disney innovation, the movie is projected on a 360-degree screen.

Carousel of Progress, like It's a Small World in Fantasyland, grew out of an attraction designed by Disney for the 1964-65 New York World's Fair. The simulated space trip of Mission to Mars was developed in cooperation with NASA. Circle-Vision 360's "American Journeys" surrounds you with the sights and sounds gathered on a thrilling tour of all 50 states in the Union.

Like true sports cars, the vehicles of the Grand Prix Raceway have disc brakes and rack-and-pinion steering. Their maximum speed, however, is only about seven miles an hour, but on the winding track, seven sometimes seems like 70. The trick in driving is to know how to steer the zippy little cars.

StarJets, an exciting high-speed adventure, whirl, rise and fall like space modules hovering around a pylon, which is modeled on a Saturn Five launch vehicle. Each jet shuttles two guests on a dizzying whirl at 11 rotations a minute above Tomorrowland. Reaching speeds of up to 26 miles an hour, the jets rise up to 80 feet above ground, displaying a view of the Magic Kingdom.

A Walt Disney World Mark IV Monorail train glides past the futuristic spires of Space Mountain gleaming in the afternoon sun. Another of the transportation forms of the future, the monorail uses about one fourth the energy of automobiles. It travels along a guideway that is suspended as much as 65 feet above ground level, and links the Magic Kingdom with EPCOT Center.

EPCOT® Center

EPCOT Center–*Future World*

A sun-spangled geosphere stands as the regal entrance to Future World and EPCOT Center. Beyond this architectural wonder, the dominions of Future World literally know no bounds. We venture back in time to the dawn of recorded history before being propelled to the sunrise of another future. We explore the depths of the oceans, traverse the land, and race toward the farthest reaches of space.

Dynamic themes are the driving forces of Future World, and each pavilion is a dazzling statement about the subject it presents.

Spaceship Earth

Spaceship Earth is the world's largest geosphere, 180 feet in diameter, and rises 18 stories above the Florida earth. It dominates the EPCOT Center skyline, its outside skin of polished aluminum reflecting the sunshine or the colorful night lighting. The geosphere's unique method of construction enables it to be stable without use of any interior supports.

Who are we? Where have we come from? Where are we going? These are the questions posed to guests in Spaceship Earth.

Housed in the spectacular EPCOT Center geosphere, Spaceship Earth serves as the theme show for all of Future World. It graphically illustrates the importance of communications to man's survival, and to his future. Spaceship Earth is more than a story about our ancestors. It's about us, our evolution, our achievements and our future responsibilities.

Following a story line conceived specifically for Spaceship Earth by eminent science-fiction author Ray Bradbury, we take a journey through time unlike any ever experienced or imagined. Spiralling gently upward through the geosphere, Time Machine vehicles take us back to the beginning of communication, back to a Cro-Magnon cave where man first began recording events on a wall. As we move through time, viewing the Audio-Animatronics show, we see this first writing surface take on different forms and shapes.

Advancing thousands of years to the New Kingdom of Egypt, we see papyrus invented, making the "wall" portable. In the ninth century B.C., the Phoenicians invent the alphabet, making written communication available to the common people as well as the wealthy. And on through the history of communication we travel, from the days of the Roman Empire through the Middle Ages, to the revolutionary introduction of the Gutenberg printing press.

The captivating ride aboard the Time Machine vehicles takes us through the history of communication. We see the first crude cave paintings, the beginnings of language, the invention of the printing press and modern computerized information storage and retrieval. This awe-inspiring presentation serves to remind us that we are fellow passengers on the spaceship we call Earth. It will be our opportunity to make it a better place through effectively using and sharing our knowledge.

Once movable type has been invented, the evolution of communication gathers speed. With the Age of Invention, new communication technologies develop at an incredibly swift pace. Vignettes show Time Travelers these developments, from steam-powered presses through the harnessing of electricity to today's—and tomorrow's—communication systems.

To this point, the Time Machines have been ascending into the dome of Spaceship Earth. Before beginning their descent, the vehicles turn, and we see the blue and white oasis of Earth against the dark and mysterious star-sprinkled galaxies. For the first time, we see our planet as it really is—a traveling spaceship.

This is the Spaceship Earth experience—a voyage that fills its travelers with an insight into man's evolution, from the dawn of our yesterday to the sunrise of our tomorrow. The narrator's parting words sum up the challenge of the future: "Tomorrow's world approaches, so let us listen and learn, let us explore and question and understand. Let us go forth and discover the wisdom to guide great Spaceship Earth through the uncharted seas of the future. Let us dare to fulfill our destiny."

A sophisticated communication center manned by Audio-Animatronics figures exemplifies modern communications technology. Here we watch computer-enhanced images, thermography, microcircuitry and computer graphics and animation. Today we receive and process an awesome amount of information, all of which can be applied to making our lives safer, happier and more productive.

CommuniCore

Thanks to rapid advancements in the areas of science and technology, the future holds an exciting and limitless array of possibilities for the improvement of human life. As with any sudden or technological change, anxieties can occur. People are unsure about these changes, or feel intimidated by futuristic, seemingly complex systems.

CommuniCore offers us the opportunity to deal with advanced technology on an individual level. The exhibits are aimed at making us feel comfortable with computers and other implements of high technology.

CommuniCore, the entrance complex to Future World, is a hub of information, entertainment and science. Within its crescent-shaped glass walls are a variety of displays, exhibits, and hands-on experiences.

Computer wizards bring backstage "on stage" every day in the Backstage Magic show, which uses animation, special effects and electronic magic to untangle the complicated world of computer technology. In the process, these mysterious machines become a little less intimidating and a little more familiar. Our hosts, EPCOT Computer Central hostess Julie and I/O, a little ball of energy who symbolizes the input and output modes of computers, show examples of the many ways we come in contact with computers at Walt Disney World, from the electronic brains in Space Mountain's mission control to computerized order-taking at fast-food restaurants.

The Energy Exchange involves guests in energy-related concepts such as solar and nuclear energy. At the Electronic Forum, a modern newsroom broadcasting from around the world, guests can voice their opinions on timely issues in a unique EPCOT Poll.

FutureCom features techniques in information via signs, satellites, newspapers and telephones, while TravelPort suggests vacation destinations around the world with touch-sensitive video screens. At the EPCOT Outreach Center, researchers use computers to answer questions from guests who want to know more about any of the subjects and technologies showcased at EPCOT Center. The Centorium offers contemporary merchandise, and the Stargate and Sunrise Terrace restaurants provide refreshments.

In CommuniCore East's Energy Exchange, touch-sensitive video screens (above) help us understand the world of energy. SMRT-1 (top) is a little robot in CommuniCore East who asks guests off-the-wall questions. Other "theatrically-inclined" robots entertain guests with an amazing display of computerized dexterity in Expo Robotics (right). In CommuniCore West, in FutureCom, we see the complexities of our telephone communication network (below).

Universe of Energy

Raging winds, steam, the surging seas, the earth's own heat, fossil fuels, nuclear fusion — the raw and basic forces that power our world are encountered and explored within Universe of Energy. An electrifying show takes us on an adventurous trek that delves into the amazing facets of energy — the heartbeat of our planet.

The formation of fossil fuels is re-enacted in a drama featuring life-sized dinosaurs which eventually become coal and oil.

The roof of Universe of Energy is covered with two acres of photovoltaic cells, which convert sunlight directly into electrical energy, providing some 15 percent of the power required to run the attraction within. Another technological wonder is found inside: The ride vehicles, which weigh about 30,000 pounds when loaded, are guided through the attraction by a wire only one-eighth inch thick, embedded in the floor. After the Audio-Animatronics presentation on present-day fuel sources, we are treated to a fascinating motion picture about sources of energy for the future.

Next, on a screen stretching 220° around us, we are immersed in an exciting live-action film dealing with today's energy challenges and the technologies that may power our tomorrows. We discover the staggering tasks involved in the search and recovery of fossil fuels, the enormous effort it took to build the Alaskan pipeline, and the almost overwhelming task of delivering the world's oil via supertanker.

For the Universe of Energy finale, images and colors move and change, creating a total energy experience and summarizing our energy possibilities. This show reemphasizes the theme that, by working together and exploring new energy frontiers, we can build a bridge to a more secure energy future.

The show in Theater I is a startlingly realistic Audio-Animatronics portrayal of the primeval world, complete with dinosaurs, eerie sounds and smells of the swamp. As we glide along, we see stegosaurus and allosaurus (opposite), pteranodon (top), a family of brontosaurus (left) and ancient dimetrodon (above). The remains of these creatures, and of the plants that nourished them, became fossil fuels.

Wonders of Life

The intricate, amazing workings of the human body and brain and the miracle of life are celebrated in the Wonders of Life, the newest pavilion in Future World at EPCOT Center. The 100,000 square-foot pavilion houses a fascinating and festive collection of life and health-related attractions designed to inspire and inform.

Body Wars sweeps visitors into a microscopic and wonderful world on a race through the human body. Innovative technology uses 70 millimeter motion picture footage projected inside a theatre that is actually a moveable flight simulator like those used to train pilots.

Next, guests will chuckle at Cranium Command, a humorous multimedia show exploring the relationship between the mind and the body as experienced by a "typical" twelve-year-old boy.

Much of the festive pavilion is devoted to Fitness Fairgrounds, a collection of hands-on exhibits, shows, and demonstrations. Here you can visit the Sensory Funhouse to explore sense-defying delights. Get a computer-generated analysis of personal lifestyles from the Met Lifestyle Revue and tips from a real sports pro on your golf, tennis or baseball swing at Coach's Corner.

Enjoy being Goofy About Health, at a multiscreen video presentation starring the Goof himself. Applaud The AnaComical Players, an improvisational theater troupe presenting comedy skits with health-related themes. And watch the miracle of human birth in a lyrical and amusing film enhanced by the magnificent work of Swedish photographer and cinematographer, Lennart Nilsson.

The picture of health is completed with a snack shop serving healthy treats and Well & Goods, Limited, where guests can shop for health-related merchandise.

The Wonders of Life links current and future developments in health sciences to daily life in dozens of informative, thought-provoking—and inspiring—ways.

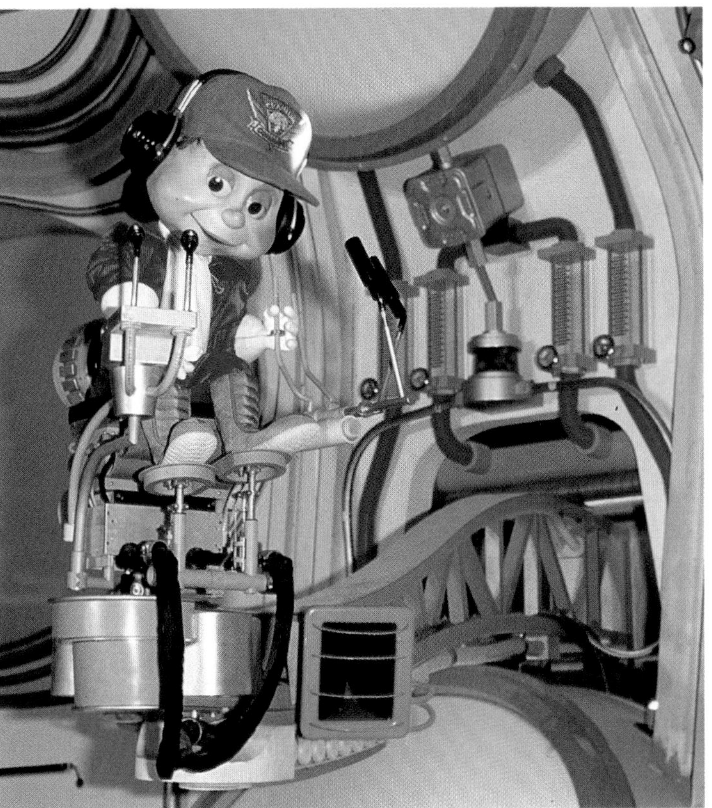

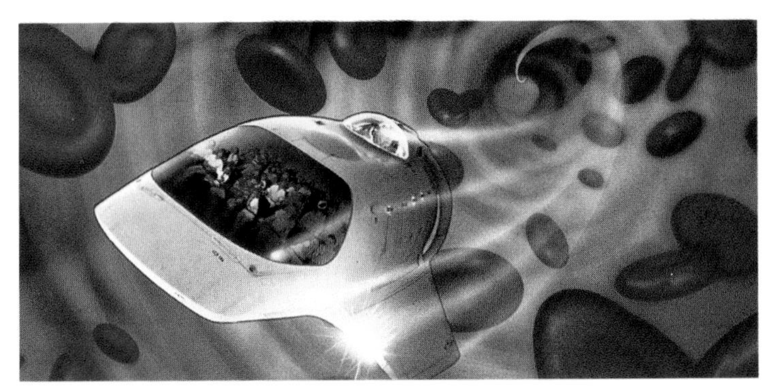

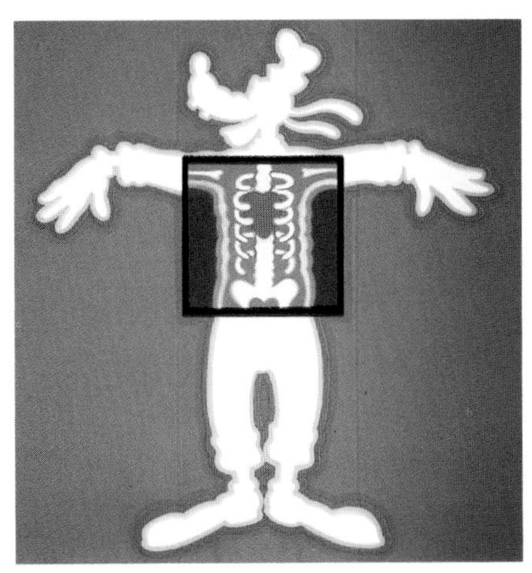

Horizons

Housed in a building that looks like a gigantic gem, Horizons is a bright view of what is in store for our future. A galaxy of pioneering visual effects show future cityscapes, space colonies, floating cities and desert farms.

Before entering the future, we see today's world as we've never seen it before. The incredible OmniSphere presents microworlds of crystal formation and chains of DNA. OmniSphere also shows macroworlds — a fiery space shuttle blast-off and intriguing extraterrestrial locales.

On tomorrow's horizons we find a 21st-century habitat beneath the sea. Here, school children equip themselves with recirculation gills for a field trip to an undersea kelp farm.

In a desert community of the future, voice-controlled robots are seen harvesting genetically engineered crops. We also visit space colonists who live within the interior of a sphere that rotates to simulate the pull of gravity. To bring members of the family together from ocean, urban, desert and space habitats, colonists use a holographic televiewer, one of tomorrow's many innovations for a better life.

Before leaving the 21st century, we choose our own tomorrow by simply pressing one of the buttons aboard the ride vehicle. Our probe of the future culminates in a simulated ride through one of the environments we've just viewed — ocean, desert or space.

In times past, man used to imagine what life would be like in the future. Jules Verne (above right) envisioned bullet-shaped rockets that would fly us to the moon. Later science-fiction writers theorized that one day all work, from kitchen chores (top) to barber services (above left) would be performed by robots. The future may be even more amazing than anything we see in Looking Back at Tomorrow. Horizons also shows us a farm of the future (opposite, bottom) and the construction of a satellite in space.

As we pass by Tomorrow's Windows, Horizons shows us captivating views of lifestyles in the future (below). We see how people would live in the zero-gravity environment of a free-floating space colony, Brava Centauri (left). Nova Cite, a fantastic metropolis, is seen from the windows of an urban apartment (above). At Sea Castle, a vast floating city in the Pacific, youngsters regularly take field trips to robot-manned sea farms (right). At Mesa Verde, a desert agricultural complex, we watch a farmer prepare a cake in his electronic pantry (below right).

World of Motion

The quest to push back the boundaries of time and space by expanding our own mobility has, through thousands of years of continual development, transformed our enormous Earth into the accessible global village it is today.

To experience World of Motion is to trace the development of transportation from man's first form of mobility, foot power, up to present and possible future methods. World of Motion begins with a rollicking journey that captures the essence of transportation history through the largest *Audio-Animatronics* show ever produced by Disney.

The World of Motion show takes a humorous look at the history of transportation. We see the first wheel factory, a Roman used chariot lot, and the beginning of the Age of Flight, as a brave balloonist soars over the rooftops of London with a cargo of pigs, goats and chickens. The show culminates in the world's first traffic jam.

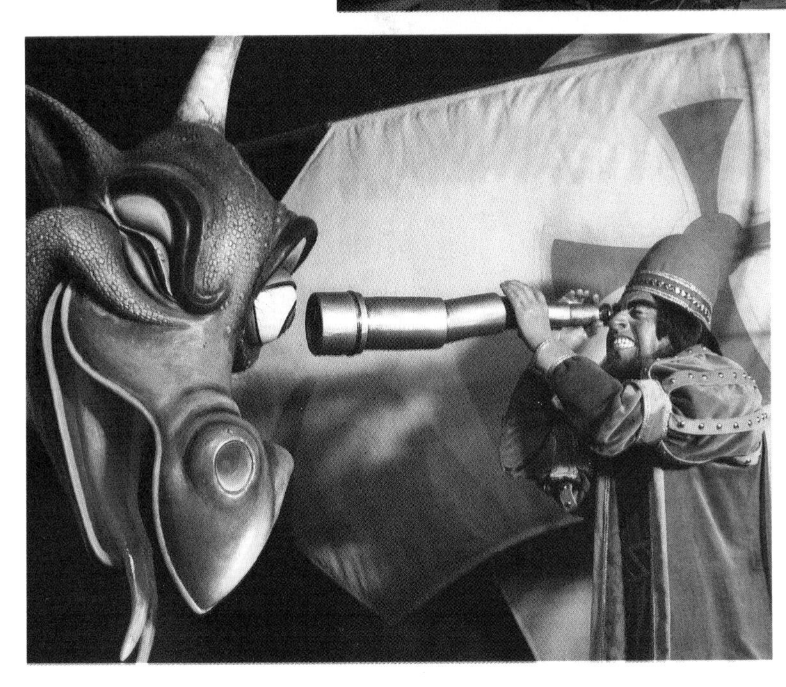

The Transcenter completes the World of Motion experience with five main exhibit areas. Aerotest dramatically demonstrates air flow patterns and their effect on fuel economy and automotive design. Bird and the Robot is a comic presentation about state-of-the-art robots working in industry. The Water Engine, an animated argument among nine cartoon characters, concerns the pros and cons of several types of internal combustion engines. Concept 2000 looks at the most advanced automobile design procedures. And Dreamer's Workshop presents designs for future technologies.

World of Motion encourages all of us to look to the future of transportation with interest, hope and optimism.

Transcenter is full of entertaining displays about the automobile, this century's most important form of transportation. It features such innovations as the Lean Machine, which can go from zero to 60 in seven seconds, the Aero 2000, which shows the beneficial effect of aerodynamics on fuel economy, and a coal-burning engine.

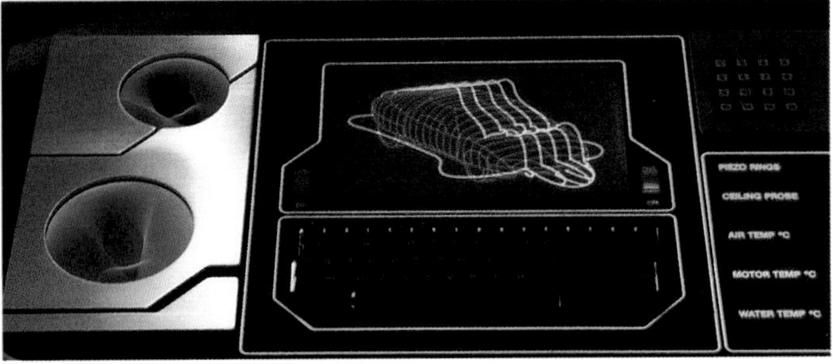

The Dreamer's Workshop shows us sleek prototype cars of the future. And in other Transcenter displays, we can watch an automobile design take shape in computer-assisted graphics, a General Motors "torture" test for new cars, and a humorous look at robots on the assembly line in the "Bird and the Robot" show.

Journey into Imagination

The human imagination is one of the most powerful and mysterious forces in the universe. Although no one really understands the process of imagination, it is the wellspring of creativity. Our ability to imagine and create is the source of all our achievement and progress.

Journey into Imagination uses the Disney tools of magic, fantasy and enchantment to remind us that all of our accomplishments begin with ideas.

Journey into Imagination is housed in a striking pavilion of quirky geometric shapes. The building itself is made of triangles of glass. One of its fountains, the "leap-frog fountain" in the picture garden, is an electronically controlled marvel that squirts one-inch streams of water from planter to planter, sometimes even over the heads of startled but delighted guests.

Journey into Imagination's four-acre area includes two towering pyramids made of mirrored glass over a tubed aluminum frame. Its spacious picture garden was designed as a relaxing area for visitors to photograph friends and family, and as a setting for some whimsical fountains. The garden's watery attractions include the Jelly Fish Fountain (top and above), where jets of water shoot up to four feet before breaking off and leaving shapes that look like flying jellyfish hanging in the air, and the Upside Down Waterfall, where water seems to "fall" uphill.

Imagination is something that is shared by all. Journey into Imagination demonstrates that we need only learn to unlock imagination and use the elements that surround us to find new solutions to the problems and challenges of tomorrow.

The metaphorical world of Journey into Imagination would not have been complete without characters to populate it, characters who could tell the story in a natural way, without lecturing. To accomplish this, the designers created what are probably the two most memorable characters in EPCOT Center—Dreamfinder and Figment.

Dreamfinder is a jolly, bearded gentleman who represents the mature, accomplished side of imagination, but who has never lost his curiosity and willingness to explore. Figment is a little dragon who embodies the impatient, questioning side of imagination that is usually associated with childhood.

Journey into Imagination, with its appeal to dreams and childlike wonder, conveys the idea that imagination is the key to creative and technical advancements. The ability to imagine and create is essential to our future survival, and can enhance our enjoyment of the present, as well.

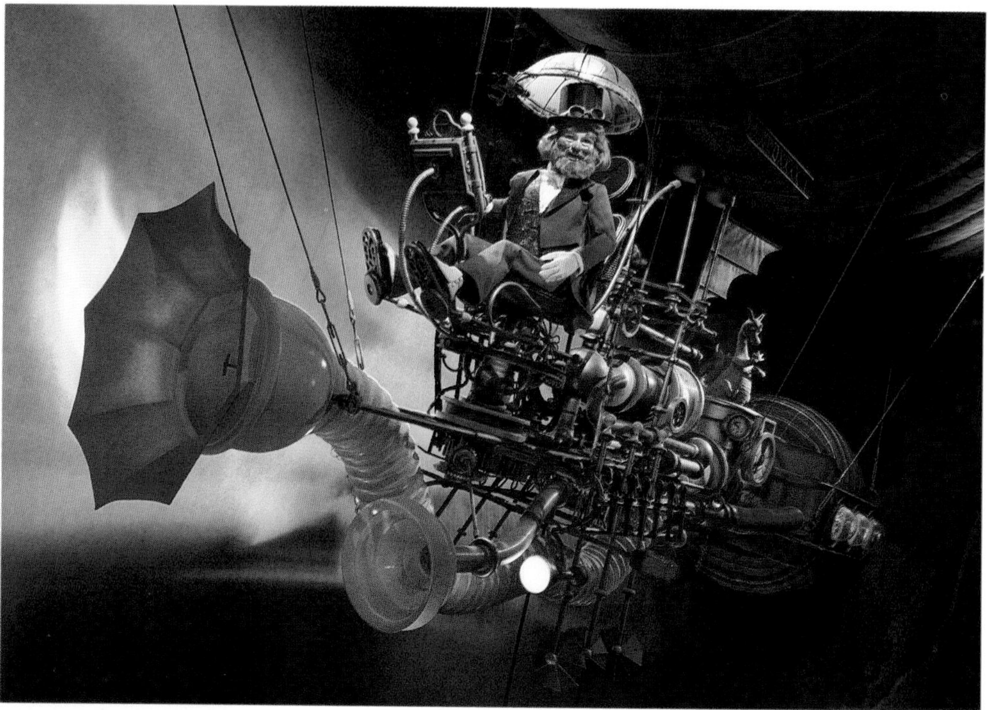

Our hosts for Journey into Imagination are Dreamfinder, a jolly, red-bearded professor, and Figment, a mischievous purple dragon, who is fashioned from the horns of a steer, royal purple pigment, and a dash of childish delight. Together they take us on an exploration of everyday elements that, when touched by imagination, combine into weird and wonderful things.

In the Image Works, we can experience the delightful fruits of imagination. We walk through color in the Rainbow Corridor (above right), and make music with our feet on Stepping Tones (above left). Journey into Imagination also houses "Captain EO," a thrilling 3-D musical space fantasy starring Michael Jackson and a cast of charming new Disney-created characters.

The Land

The Land is Future World's salute to the earth. It includes areas where revolutionary growing methods are presented as part of the solution to feeding the people of tomorrow. Also in The Land are two restaurants, The Land Grille Room and the Farmer's Market, where good nutrition and good taste go hand in hand.

The largest of the Future World structures, The Land encompasses nearly six acres. It is comprised of several attractions, research facilities and restaurants. The Land explores man's relationship to nature and the land, and his never-ending quest for a means to feed the people of the world.

In The Land, we can participate in a boat trip, take a guided walking tour through growing areas, see a motion picture about the delicate balance between technology and the environment and enjoy a humorous *Audio-Animatronics* show about the benefits of good nutrition.

In Listen to the Land, we set off on a boat cruise through a rain forest, a desert and a prairie. Each of these "biomes" is experienced in all its beauty and harshness.

A guided tour through The Land's growing areas gives us detailed descriptions of such strategies as hydroponics, intercropping and aquaculture. There is even a demonstration of a method of growing plants that can be adapted to space—a revolving drum that will simulate gravity in a gravity-free environment.

The Tomorrow's Harvest Tour is a guided walking tour of the growing areas of The Land. This tour includes a look at a future farm, where we explore such innovations in agriculture as a zero-gravity lettuce drum, Halophyte racks, spray boxes and column posts. Also seen on the tour are an intensive crop reproduction area, desert and tropical agriculture, and the Aqua Cell.

Kitchen Kabaret, an *Audio-Animatronics* show set in an enormous kitchen, tells us through a cabaret-like show a story of the benefits of good nutrition. Featured players include Bonnie Appetit, the hostess; a house band called the Kitchen Krackpots; the Cereal Sisters, Mairzy Oats, Rennie Rice and Connie Corn; a Latin band called the Colander Combo; and Mr. Dairy Goods and his Stars of the Milky Way, the Misses Cheese, Yogurt and Ice Cream.

The Land tells the story of man's beneficial interaction with his environment. By taking a look at our past efforts to tame the land, and theorizing about our future endeavors, The Land promotes the belief that nature's resources can be efficiently utilized to meet the food needs of the future.

In the Listen to the Land boat tour, we glide through a South American rain forest, where harvesting food is the challenge; the African Desert, where the problem is the availability of water; and the American plains (above), where hot summers and cold winters are the conditions that must be taken into account in farming.

Each of the acts of Kitchen Kabaret focuses on one of the four basic food groups – meats and proteins, dairy products, fruits and vegetables, and grains and cereals. The jokes are corny and the characters endearing; they make the good-nutrition message an easy one to swallow. As Bonnie Appetit says in the finale, "Proper foods each time you dine can keep you fit and feelin' fine. Eating right's a healthy sign."

The Living Seas

Through eight-inch-thick acrylic observation windows, we watch as human divers go about the business of feeding and studying the creatures of The Living Seas. The 15-foot-deep marine mammals pool (above right) allows us to watch researchers as they conduct various studies involving dolphins and sea lions. Television monitors show us what is happening under water whenever a diver with a television camera or a video-equipped mini-sub is in the environment.

The seas are a dominant feature of our planet, unique in our solar system. Together, they cover three quarters of the world's surface. Within their depths are mysteries man has only begun to recognize.

The Living Seas is dedicated to the exploration and understanding of this vast realm. It houses a self-contained ocean environment, the largest of its kind in the world, with over 200 varieties of Caribbean coral-reef sealife, from tiny zooplankton to enormous sharks.

Within The Living Seas we also find Seabase Alpha, a high-tech, 21st-century oceanic research base. Among its features are state-of-the-art undersea exploration techniques and fascinating demonstrations by human-dolphin research teams.

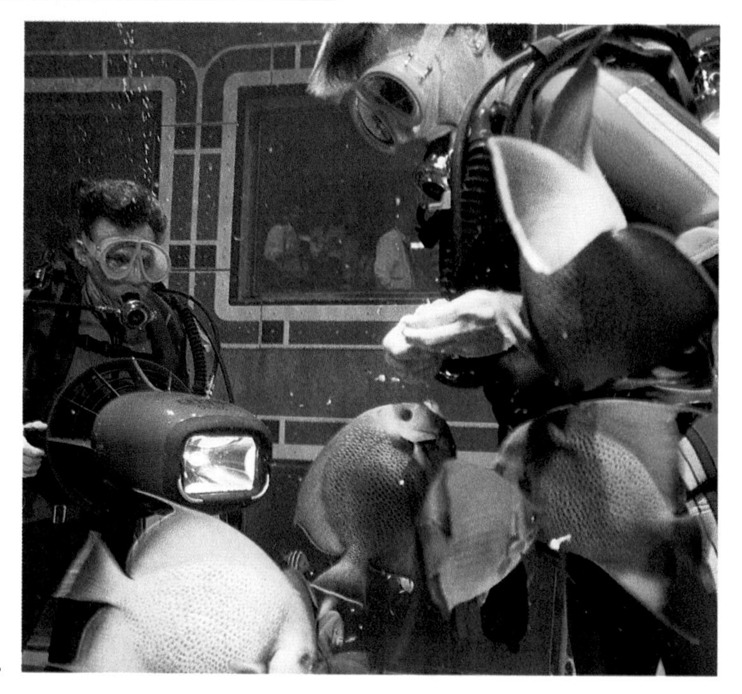

The Living Seas' self-contained coral reef tank is a six million-gallon "ocean," 27 feet deep and 203 feet across—so wide that it is sometimes difficult to see across it. Here, in a unique man-made environment, we watch researchers conduct experiments we can usually read about only in scientific journals.

Other exhibits and interactive experiences include a Pacific coast kelp forest, Pacific lagoon tide pool, a 24-foot wave machine, the lock-out chamber used by divers to enter and leave the main tank, and Seabase Challenge, which invites us to test our knowledge of the ocean.

Many more exciting experiences await the visitor to The Living Seas. They explain the past and present status of man's relationship with the oceans which surround us, and give us tantalizing glimpses of the promise that relationship holds for the future.

Visitors to Seabase Alpha are fascinated by the 22-1/2-foot Scuba Tube (left), which gives divers access to The Living Seas' underwater research station. It takes 60 seconds to fill the tube with water, and 42 seconds to drain it. The JIM Suit (above) allows humans to work at depths as low as 1,500 feet without danger of decompression. A cutaway model of the suit enables guests to try working with its manipulator hands.

Mickey Mouse (top right) was a special guest at the opening of The Living Seas. A gourmet dining experience awaits guests of the Coral Reef Restaurant (above), where the quality of the seafood and the creativity of its preparation make for a memorable meal.

EPCOT Center–*World Showcase*

It would take a lifetime of vacations to explore the many countries of the world. For travelers to EPCOT Center's World Showcase, however, the dream of world travel comes true.

Here, amid nations standing in friendship beside a broad lagoon, we meet gaily-costumed young people who have actually come from the World Showcase countries. It is their charm and friendliness that form bonds stretching to all people, everywhere.

The American Adventure

A startlingly realistic Benjamin Franklin (left) is the spokesman for The American Adventure, along with Mark Twain. The Voices of Liberty singers (below and right) entertain us with early American and patriotic songs. The finale to The American Adventure show includes the Spirits of America (bottom left), who stand for the qualities that have made America great.

Through a multitude of entertainment media, never before realized collectively on stage, we witness the events that shaped America, the land of freedom.

The American Adventure combines large-screen projection with inspiring music and special effects. It also presents performances by the most lifelike *Audio-Animatronics* figures ever developed. Benjamin Franklin and Mark Twain, two of America's most eloquent spokesmen, lead a cast of more than 35 full-sized historic performers. Franklin actually walks in this show, a major milestone in *Audio-Animatronics* imagineering.

With its deep-seated patriotism and acknowledgement of the contributions of all men, The American Adventure stands as the unification of World Showcase.

THE AMERICAN

Mexico

Within the majestic pyramid of Mexico lie artifacts from her colorful history, as well as bold new emblems of a country moving proudly into the future.

Folkloric groups from Veracruz and Yucatan perform their festive numbers as flower-laden boats whisk us off on a cruise through the rich heritage of ancient, colonial and modern Mexico.

Time peels away as a life-size stone image of a Mayan priest magically comes to life to welcome us. Dancers and unusual music weave a tale of Mayan, Toltec and Aztec history.

Songs of celebration then fill the wind and children play and dance to modern Mexican music. The boat then glides into the resort areas of Mexico for a holiday on film, before we're bid a fond "Adios!" in a shower of fireworks.

The pyramid structure that houses Mexico was inspired by Meso-American architecture dating from the third century, A.D.

The pre-Columbian mask at left is a fine example of the changing art exhibits to be found inside the pyramid.

The serpent heads (top left) that decorate the Mexico pyramid represent the Aztec god Quetzalcoatl, while mariachi musicians exemplify a colorful part of present-day Mexican culture. The San Angel Inn, where authentic Mexican gourmet cuisine is served, is modeled after the famous restaurant of the same name in Mexico City. The Inn serves especialidades like Mole Poblano (chicken simmered in 20 Mexican spices and a hint of chocolate) and Huachinango a la Veracruzana (red snapper poached in wine with onions, tomato and Mexican peppers).

Norway

From traditional legends to modern technology, a proud past and future come together in Norway, where visitors travel through time on a tumultuous voyage along craggy fjords, then take a widescreen film tour of the land of the midnight sun today.

Guests find a friendly welcome as they explore a picturesque town square designed to represent the Norwegian towns and cities of Bergen, Oslo, Alesund and Setesdahl. Here they can find fine Norwegian crafts in "The Puffin Roost" and "The Fjordling," sample Scandinavian pastries and sandwiches at a charming open cafe and bakery or enjoy hearty Nordic fare in the Akershus restaurant with its medieval banquet hall.

A stone replica of the Akershus, a 14th-century fortress, stands guard over the cobblestone courtyard of a picturesque town square.

A traditional wooden stave church (right) is among the many authentic architectural styles represented in Norway. Travelers on the "Maelstrom: A High Seas Norwegian Adventure," (below) sail on dragon-headed boats past a tenth-century Viking village, through a shadowy mythical forest guarded by trolls and water spirits, and down raging waterfalls.

China

From the moment we pass through the ceremonial gate of China, the mystery and serenity of this ancient country is felt. Three towering rocks stand at the entrance, looking much like the ones with which ancient rulers ornamented their ceremonial palaces. The beautiful waterfalls, reflecting ponds and gardens further enhance the atmosphere of peace and tranquility.

As important to the Chinese as nature and serenity is their Hall of Prayer for Good Harvests, which stands majestically as the focal point of the showcase. Through this lovely, three-tiered temple we enter a theater where the Circle-Vision 360 film "Wonders of China: Land of Beauty, Land of Time" is shown. It is narrated by Li Bai, an ancient poet who guides the audience through China's history, culture and breathtaking scenery. In just twenty minutes, we experience the Great Wall, the Forbidden City, Mongolia, the Summer Palace and the Yangtze River, to name only a few sights.

Traditional Chinese banners at the entrance to China proclaim "May virtue be your neighbor," and "May good fortune follow you on your path through life." Inside, traditional Chinese tranquility prevails, fostered by the soothing tones of Chinese music, the perfection of the landscaping and the timeless quality of the architecture. In the House of the Whispering Willows (top) is a breathtaking Circle-Vision 360 film about a land few of us have ever seen. The Nine Dragons Restaurant (above left) serves succulent Peking duck, as well as provincial cuisine.

Unlocking the beauties and mysteries of China to create awe-inspiring film was not an easy task. Some areas of China were so difficult to reach that equipment had to be brought in on camelback. At one location, a 300-pound camera had to be hand-carried up 16,700 steps.

With its distinctive landscaping, detailed architecture and peaceful setting, China is successfully captured within World Showcase. And all who visit gain an appreciation and understanding of the country, its people, its customs, its art and its culture.

Germany

A land of fantasy, folklore and festivity, Germany entices visitors with its splendid scenery, enchants them with its storybook-like cities and excites them with its spirited celebrations.

When asked what comes to mind when we think of Germany, we are likely to mention picturesque villages, romantic castles and lively beer gardens. Undoubtedly we will think of the exquisite Black Forest, named for the majestic trees that cover that region. All the excitement and enchantment of this fairy-tale country is captured in Germany at World Showcase.

The moment we enter Germany, the castle in the distance, the rustic store fronts and the melodic ringing of a carillon transport us to the heart of Bavaria. On the cobblestone platz, gingerbread-style shops, a clock tower, a statue of St. George slaying the dragon and the far-off castle present an idealized village. Adding to the total atmosphere of Germany are the charming costumes of the hosts and hostesses.

In Germany's St. Georgsplatz is a statue of St. George slaying the legendary dragon. From time to time, typical German music is performed in this plaza, which draws its architectural inspiration from many German towns.

True to its name, Der Bücherwurm (top right) sells books, classic and contemporary. Here we also find sheet music by the great German composers, as well as reproductions of works by noted German painters, and originals by contemporary artists. In Glas und Porzellan (above left), you can often find artists at work creating the famous Hummel figurines. In the Biergarten Restaurant (above right and below), you can always find hearty cuisine and merriment. And in Porzellanhaus (below right), you probably won't be able to resist the magnificently detailed porcelain animals and birds.

Italy

Playful gondolas and their barber-striped moorings reflect the world of romance and classic grace that is Italy.

We are invited to begin a love affair with Venice as we stand in the shadows of the breathtaking Campanile, or bell tower, in St. Mark's Square.

A re-creation of the Doge's Palace stands at one side of the square, flanked by the well-known Lion of St. Mark sculpture. Inside the palace is a treasure trove of fine art, jewelry and crystal, and a wealth of culinary delights.

In the Piazza del Teatro we find the outdoor provincial theater, where Commedia dell'Arte players and Carnival in Venice dancers perform in the finest tradition of their arts.

A visit to the Italy showcase is a truly memorable experience for all who have listened to its alluring song.

As befits a re-creation of Venice, one of Italy's most romantic and culturally distinct cities, the Italy showcase's architecture and decoration are faithfully exact replicas of their original models, if somewhat scaled down. The intricate facade of the Doge's Palace (left) is executed in authentic marble, while the angel atop the Campanile (above) is covered in genuine gold leaf.

Italy's restaurant (top left), a version of the renowned Alfredo's in Rome, is designed in the Florentine style. Its interior walls are covered with trompe l'oeil ("fool the eye") paintings copied from those of Veronese. Street players (top right) perform daily in the Piazza del Teatro, while during Italy's Worldfest celebration (above), entertainment also includes folk dancers and singers. Fountains can be found everywhere in Italy, many of them designed by the nation's most prominent artists. The Fontana di Nettuno in the Italy Showcase (below) is modeled after one by Bernini, and exemplifies the massive and elaborate style of many Italian fountains.

Japan

Japan is often noted for its modern technology, bustling cities and dynamic society. However, today's Japan has its roots in precious cultural values that have remained constant throughout centuries. These are an appreciation of beauty, a reverence for knowledge and learning, and a devotion to the arts. It is these values that are reflected in World Showcase's Japan.

In Japan, gardening is a precise art, and every object and its placement have special meaning. Careful consideration is given to the placement of rocks, water elements, evergreens and decorative lanterns.

The pagoda that so symbolizes Japan (far right) was modeled after one in Nara that dates from the seventh century, the lovely Horyuji temple. Its five stories represent, from top to bottom, earth, water, fire, wind and sky. This goju-no-to stands 83 feet high, and is surmounted by a sorin, or spire, composed of nine rings, each with its own wind chimes.

Japanese architecture shows the knowledge and ancient customs that have been carried down through the centuries. In the Japan showcase we find a representative sampling of traditional structures, including a Torii and a five-story pagoda.

The landscaping also reflects ancient Japanese traditions. Rocks represent the enduring nature of the earth. Water, in the form of a stream and pools of colorful koi fish, is a symbol of the sea, the source of life. The evergreen trees that grow so lushly here symbolize eternal life.

Overall, with its breathtaking gardens, ornate structures and depiction of a rich cultural heritage, the mystique and graciousness that exemplify Japan come to life for us in this stunning showcase.

The bright vermillion torii *(gate) (left) that is the entranceway to Japan from World Showcase Lagoon is derived from the design of a gate at the ancient Itsukushima Shrine in Hiroshima Bay. Its form resembles a Japanese calligraphic character.*

Morocco

Native Moroccan dancers (above) performed at the dedication of Morocco during Worldfest in 1984. Throughout this striking showcase, we see the intricate geometric patterns used by Islamic artists in place of the animals and birds often portrayed by their Western counterparts.

It is called the "Jewel of Africa." It is the land of Casablanca, of towering minarets and sacred mosques, of tasty *couscous* and tangy fruit concoctions.

Here in Morocco we find an intriguing blend of old and new, where age-old customs and traditions mingle with modern thoughts and innovations.

World Showcase's Morocco showcase captures the spirit and flavor of this mysterious North African nation. It is a world of spacious courtyards, narrow winding streets, intricate architecture and refreshing fountains splashing in colorful gardens.

Morocco is divided into two sections, as are most Moroccan cities. In the *ville nouvelle* (new city), we find the Royal Gallery and Tourism Information. In the Medina (old city), we find a bustling market filled with quaint shops and stunning landmarks. Here are faithful reproductions of the Bab Boujouloud gate, the Minaret at Chella, the Koutoubia Minaret, the Nejjarine Fountain and the Bells of the Madrassa.

Morocco is a captivating step back into a land steeped in tradition and rich in beauty.

Shops in the Medina offer an eye-catching array of Moroccan handicrafts, worked in wood, metal, leather and straw. This showcase is rather special, in that its intricate decorative motifs were all hand-applied by Moroccan artisans called maalems. *They work in enameled terracotta tiles or carved plaster-work. The walls, floors and ceilings of Morocco are fine examples of their ancient art.*

France

France, Europe's oldest unified nation and Western Europe's largest, has been the center of western culture for centuries, both as a major political power and as a leader in the arts and sciences. The French countryside is rich and fertile, and the country's famed capital, Paris, epitomizes beauty and grandeur.

Entering France in World Showcase, we are treated immediately to a stroll over Paris's picturesque Seine River. A park, inspired by a Georges Seurat painting, borders the canal, and chimney pots punctuate building rooftops along the boulevard. In the distance, we see a one-tenth scale reproduction of a famous landmark, the Eiffel Tower.

The charm and romance that are the hallmarks of Paris and the provinces are here to enjoy in France. Here we find mansard roofs, sidewalk cafes, elegant shops and tree-lined boulevards. Even the Seine River is here, to be crossed by a replica of the charming old Parisian footbridge that used to lead from the Louvre to the quais of the Left Bank.

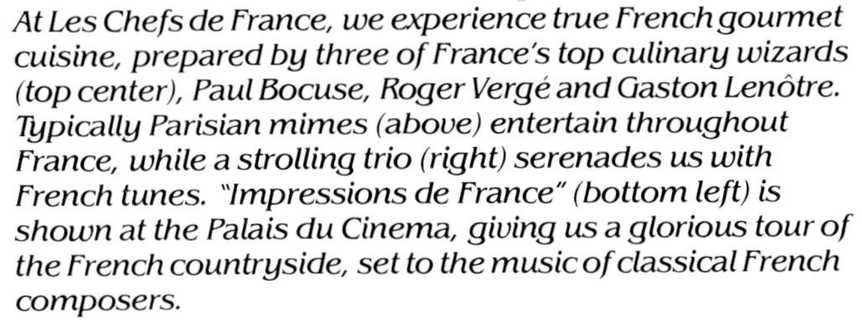

At Les Chefs de France, we experience true French gourmet cuisine, prepared by three of France's top culinary wizards (top center), Paul Bocuse, Roger Vergé and Gaston Lenôtre. Typically Parisian mimes (above) entertain throughout France, while a strolling trio (right) serenades us with French tunes. "Impressions de France" (bottom left) is shown at the Palais du Cinema, giving us a glorious tour of the French countryside, set to the music of classical French composers.

The United Kingdom

Eight different architectural styles set the mood for a tour of "merrie olde England" in the United Kingdom showcase. Buildings range from London Victorian to Yorkshire manor, Tudor to Georgian, Hyde Park and Regency to Shakespearean cottage. The entertainment here is exuberantly British. The Pearly Kings and Queens (bottom) perform traditional British music hall numbers.

Green lawns, gabled rooftops, shops along cobblestone streets and a charming waterside pub provide a typically British setting for the United Kingdom.

"United Kingdom" represents the political unity of four regions: England, Scotland, Wales and Northern Ireland. Each country has its own glorious history, but it's the essence of the empire as a whole that is captured in World Showcase.

Snuggled alongside the lagoon, the traditional pub offers fare to satisfy a king-sized appetite. On the street, we're met by energetic entertainers, including the Pearly Kings and Queens, whose comedy style is as bright as the pearly buttons sewn on their costumes.

The cool greenery of an English park lures us to pause for a moment's rest and relaxation. And for a bit more lively entertainment, music and theatricals are performed under the shade of the gazebo in the open square.

With a happy blend of architectural styles that represent 400 years of British history, the United Kingdom offers a distinct "old world" feeling of enchantment.

The chandelier in the Adams Room of the Queen's Table (above left) is made of Waterford crystal. This shop offers fine Royal Doulton china and crystal. The Renaissance Players (above right) sometimes succeed in persuading members of their audiences to join in their lively playlets. The Rose & Crown Pub and Dining Room (bottom right) is typical of Victorian England, with etched glass panels, dark mahogany bar and dart board. The Pub's bill of fare includes traditional ales and stout (served at room temperature, of course), cottage pie and bangers and mash.

Canada

The entrance to Canada winds through a replica of Victoria's famed Butchart Gardens (below), where we find brilliant flowers and Canada's beloved maple trees. Entertainment is provided by the Maple Leaf Brass Band, whose rollicking performance combines music and comedy.

From a Northwest Indian village to a 19th-century French chateau and the winding, narrow streets of Quebec City, the remarkable diversity of Canadian cultures and the awesome majesty of her wilderness are captured in Canada.

The miracle of Circle-Vision 360 takes us on a breathtaking film tour of the largest country in the Western hemisphere. We see Canadian geese take to the skies, a Calgary Stampede, downhill skiers and a dizzying aerial view from Toronto's C.N. Tower, the highest free-standing structure in the world.

Canada features the totem art of Northwest Indians (top). Five free-standing poles, which catalog family history, legends and accomplishments, soar 30 feet into the air. The Trading Post (above) offers authentic handcrafted Indian and Eskimo goods.

Canada also beckons us to take a walking tour through her exciting back country. Beyond a charming Quebec thoroughfare, we wind down a steep mountain path. We pass a river bank, footpaths and bridges, tall pine trees, rushing waterfalls and an abandoned mine tunnel from the Klondike gold rush days.

Later we see Salmon Island, where logging games are held year-round, and a Northwest Indian village. A trip through Canada is truly an awe-inspiring one; it captures the essence of Canada, today and yesterday.

IllumiNations

Blazing into life over World Showcase Lagoon, IllumiNations amazes guests nightly. A spectacular display of symphonic music and light transforms the nations of the World Showcase into a brilliant, blazing wonderland. The show took two years to create, and required hundreds of new technological developments in order to achieve its "awe-inspiring" effect.

IllumiNations takes viewers on a magical light tour of the national showcases (shown top to bottom: American Adventure, France and Germany) as each one in turn is illuminated by thousands of twinkling lights and special effects projections.

Over seven hundred individual fireworks and the coordinated efforts of twenty-five computer systems are required to work the evening enchantment of IllumiNations

Disney-MGM Studios Theme Park

Disney-MGM Studios Theme Park

Surrounding visitors with color, light and action, the Disney-MGM Studios Theme Park captures all the atmosphere and ambiance of the movies.

Here is the glamorous aura of Hollywood's golden years; the adventure and romance of famous scenes from classic films; the thrilling exploits of stunt performers and the fascinating behind-the-scenes world of film wizardry and craftsmanship.

Visitors to the Disney-MGM Studios become—not just onlookers, but participants in every exciting moment. So join the cast. Enter a world of moviemaking magic where you are one of the stars of the show!

Disney · MGM
STUDIOS

Hollywood Boulevard

From atop the Crossroads of the World, Mickey Mouse invites guests to stroll along Hollywood Boulevard where all the glamor of Hollywood's golden era is recreated in lavish detail. Reproductions of famous landmarks house inviting shops and elegant restaurants offering authentic movie memorabilia and cuisine adapted from the original menus of famed Hollywood eating places.

At its hub, the entrance to the Chinese Theatre and The Great Movie Ride beckons. Along the way, street performers create a "you are there" feeling. It's all part of the fun and fantasy made real in this mecca for movie fans.

The Great Movie Ride

The Great Movie Ride is a cinematic adventure that is like holding a visitor's pass to famous film sets and movie scenes.

Inside the Chinese Theatre, a full-scale reproduction of the facade of Hollywood's premiere movie palace, a giant cyclorama of the Hollywood Hills at sunset sets the mood for a journey into a full-scale celebration of the movies—with their power to send imaginations soaring.

Travelers through the realms of moviedom are in center stage as they view a splashy salute to Hollywood musicals, maneuver through the dark underworld of gangster flicks, dodge bullets in a classic western showdown, explore an accursed ancient temple, and narrowly escape the clutches of a bloodthirsty space creature. The fun culminates in a three-minute film tribute created by Academy Award-winning filmmaker, Chuck Workman, using scenes from over 90 well-known films.

Fabulous sets, special effects and a lively cast of live and *Audio-Animatronics* stars make each moment as real as if you had stepped into the films themselves.

Backlot Annex and Lakeside Circle

Action is at its wildest and funniest at the Backlot Annex and Lakeside Circle where do-it-yourself-fun is the name of the game!

At SuperStar Television located at Lakeside Circle, audience members are chosen to interact onstage with prerecorded film episodes from vintage and contemporary television shows. Through the magic of electronics, each performance is incorporated into the existing film and shown on overhead monitors—much to the delight of hundreds of cheering fans!

The Monster Sound Show in the Sound Effects Studio provides a hands-and-ears-on demonstration of how film sound effects are created. Audience members are invited to use the devices on a foley (sound effects) stage to add sound to a specially-produced film starring two of America's top comedians. A before-and-after screening emphasizes how much the "sound of magic" adds to any film! In addition, guests can enjoy SoundWorks, a collection of sound adventures such as Movie Mimics, Phonic Funnies and Soundsations.

Next stop for the bold-at-heart is the Indiana Jones Epic Stunt Spectacular at the Backlot Annex. Here professional stunt artists demonstrate mind-boggling escapes, fights, explosions and other tricks of the trade used in creating dramatic scenes from classic adventure films.

For those interested in adventurous dining—or just an opportunity to relax—Lakeside Circle offers unique opportunities at Min and Bill's Dockside Diner, the Tune In Lounge, 50's Prime Time Cafe or Dinosaur Gertie's Ice Cream of Extinction.

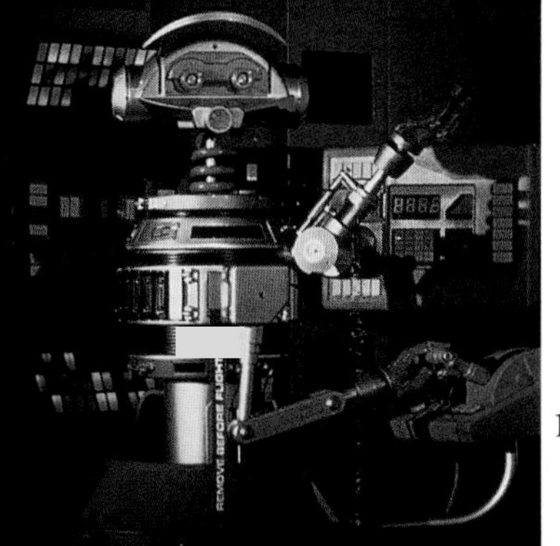

Backstage Studio Tour

The Backstage Studio Tour is part of the Production Center, a state-of-the-art facility in use since June, 1988. Here visitors go behind the scenes to experience the many aspects of actual production. From watching designers ply their craft, and traveling through full-scale, finely-detailed sets such as New York Street to seeing actual filming in progress on the massive soundstages, guests get a close-up, intimate view of the best-kept secrets of the film trade.

But that's just part of the story! For the Backstage Studio Tour also offers entertaining moments of personal participation. It's a fascinating trip into the world of filmmaking that will change the way you view films forever.

At the Water Effects Tank, guests go from sunshine to stormy weather in seconds. A battleship fights immense waves, and a tugboat plows through a storm at sea, while a torrential downpour dampens everything but the spirit of fun!

A highlight of the Backstage Studio Tour, Catastrophe Canyon treats travelers to heart-stopping disaster—complete with an earthquake, explosion, firestorm and a 30,000 gallon flash flood!

Volunteers "ride" a giant bee in the Special Effects Workshop, a kind of "mad scientist's" laboratory where skilled technicians can shrink people, create monsters and make movie magic before your eyes.

The Magic of Disney Animation

The heart of Disney has always been animation, and what better place to honor it than at the Disney-MGM Studios Theme Park! Inside The Magic of Disney Animation, guests watch animators, inkers and painters at work during a fascinating self-guided tour while video monitors provide insightful, humorous commentary.

Two theatrical presentations: "Back to Never Land," a witty overview of the animation process plus a sparkling retrospective of classic Disney animated films add to the celebration. Rare original art from the Disney archives is on view at The Disney Animation Collection, and valuable collectibles are available from the selection of lithographs, hand-painted, original cels and models at The Animation Gallery.

The Vacation Kingdom

The Vacation Kingdom

Another wealth of Disney adventure awaits us in the exciting locales surrounding the Magic Kingdom and EPCOT Center. In an area about twice the size of Manhattan, Disney has built roads, lakes, islands, canals, golf courses, shopping areas, hotels, even a small zoo.

This Vacation Kingdom is an entertainment world. Its collection of unique themed environments brings to life a number of our leisure-time dreams, whether we wish to step into the future, yearn for the exotic South Seas, or just want to rough it in the great outdoors.

Waterways of the World

From the waterways of American history comes the great white sidewheeler that ferries people across Bay Lake and the Seven Seas Lagoon. It is complete with walking-beam engines, unlike any built in the last 100 years.

Everywhere we look in the Vacation Kingdom, we see bodies of water—bays, waterfalls, lagoons, canals, ponds, trickling streams. Some of these act as aquatic highways. Others provide decorative accents or soothing background to a vacation experience like no other.

The excavation of the Seven Seas Lagoon took nearly three years. Today it spans 185 acres, embraces three islands and reaches an average depth of ten feet. The sparkling waterway offers an exciting aquatic approach to the Magic Kingdom and is a setting for water pageants and numerous recreational activities.

Bay Lake was excavated, too. Its water was simply too polluted to meet Disney standards. When refilled, Bay Lake was stocked with bass, not only providing sport for anglers, but also aiding in insect control.

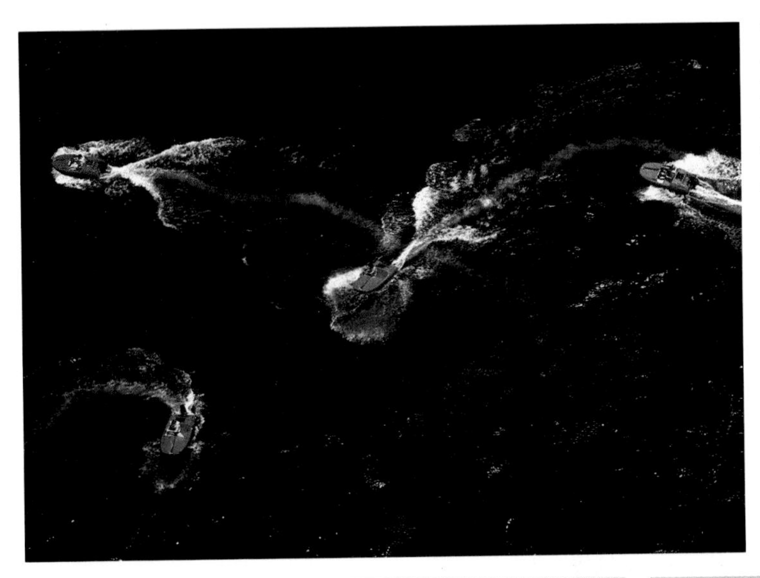

The Vacation Kingdom boasts the nation's largest fleet of pleasure craft, including sailboats, catamarans, pedal boats and mini-speedboats. Its "commercial" fleet features everything from 600-passenger, diesel-powered ferryboats to motor launches.

Normally a bridge is constructed to carry ground transportation over a body of water. But at Walt Disney World, a concrete water bridge built over a highway connects the Seven Seas Lagoon with Bay Lake. Crossing this unique bridge makes travel around the Vacation Kingdom almost as easy by water as by land.

Cruising over the waters of the Seven Seas Lagoon or Bay Lake can be great sport. The little Water Sprite speedboats are as much fun as they look. Although they don't really go that fast, their small size intensifies the feeling of speed. Other kinds of boats, for one or more persons, are available at the many marinas in Walt Disney World.

Disney's Grand Floridian Beach Resort

Considered the "jewel in the crown" of Disney's resorts, Disney's Grand Floridian Beach Resort rises like a light-hearted Victorian fantasy above the sugar-sand beaches of Seven Seas Lagoon.

Graced by gleaming white gingerbread, the 900-room resort is easily accessible by Monorail from the Magic Kingdom and EPCOT, and offers luxurious options for recreation including a marina, beach, swimming pool, children's activity area, beautifully-appointed health club and elegant shops.

The elegance of by-gone days is reflected in the lobby with its 85-foot atrium with triple stained-glass domes, open-cage elevator and aviary. (Above) Serenades by string quartets, high tea served overlooking the water, and a variety of options for distinctive dining at restaurants like Victoria and Albert's make a visit to Disney's Grand Floridian an experience in luxury at its loveliest and best.

Disney's Contemporary Resort

Praised for its imaginative design and dramatic use of space, Disney's Contemporary Resort was described by *The New York Times* as "the best single building through which to observe the blending of technological innovation and far-out fantasy that is uniquely Disney."

Enclosed within the hotel's imposing steel and concrete A-frame is an enormous open area called the Grand Canyon Concourse. It is nine stories high and the length of one and a half football fields. Rows of guest rooms open into it on both sides.

Pieced together like giant jigsaw puzzles, colossal ceramic murals (detail below) rise 90 feet from the floor of the Grand Canyon Concourse. If an evening of fine dining, dancing and entertainment is what you're looking for, don't miss "Broadway at the Top" (center right), a rousing salute to the American musical theater.

Sleek, silent monorail trains continually arrive and depart in the hotel's unique "lobby," linking it with Disney's Polynesian Resort, the Magic Kingdom and EPCOT Center.

Disney's Contemporary Resort is unique in many respects, not the least in its method of construction. Its guest rooms are prefabricated modular units that were produced three miles away and transported to the construction site. There each unit was hoisted by a giant crane and slid into the hotel's steel frame like a drawer into a bureau.

The impressive and spacious Contemporary Resort offers dining, dancing and entertainment at its Top of the World supper club, as well as sandy beaches, a marina and night-lighted tennis courts.

Disney's Polynesian Resort

Resting on the shores of the Seven Seas Lagoon, Disney's Polynesian Resort offers white beaches trimmed with palm trees, crystalline swimming pools, and a fleet of watercraft for gliding lazily along.

Lush landscaping and an air of relaxed comfort characterize this hotel. A miniature rain forest flourishes within the Great Ceremonial House. Sunlight and moonlight stream onto waterfalls, volcanic rock formations and towering coconut palms. This jungle features more than 75 botanical species, including nearly 1,500 orchids, gardenias and banana trees.

One of the Vacation Kingdom's most popular nightspots is Luau Cove, where the Polynesian Revue features authentic island delicacies and a cast of Polynesian performers.

"Aitea-Peatea," promises the Polynesian Resort's motto: "There will be another day tomorrow just like today." This restful resort's mood is one of calm relaxation. Nothing is ever rushed or hectic here, where white sand beaches beckon and palm fronds wave.

The natives may feel restless, but guests don't, as they enjoy colorful performances of authentic South Sea dances, try their skill at maneuvering outrigger canoes, enjoy the lushly landscaped tropical waterfalls, or browse through shops full of exotic merchandise.

The Disney Inn

Nestled into a quiet corner of the Walt Disney World landscape is The Disney Inn. It features two 18-hole, par-72 championship courses.

Tight fairways and elevated greens, generously punctuated with water hazards and sand traps, make these courses a challenge to amateurs and professionals alike.

The Disney Inn's 400 acres were carefully planned for golf enjoyment, ecologically sound soil management and retention of natural beauty. The Magnolia course is lined with 1,000 magnolia trees, while the Palm course is embraced by 1,000 palms of ten varieties.

Water hazards on the course do double duty as irrigation stores. Soil displaced from ponds and canals during construction has been used to elevate greens and tees.

Four different tees are available on all holes, so that golfers of varying skill levels can find challenge without frustration.

The Magnolia course is the site of the final round of the annual Walt Disney World National Team Championship Pro Am tournament.

The Disney Inn also offers a full-service Pro Shop, as well as swimming, tennis and fine dining in the comfortable Garden Gallery.

The Walt Disney World Open was played on The Disney Inn's championship courses in 1971, 1972 and 1973. Winner of all three tournaments was Jack Nicklaus (above). Sand traps dot both the Magnolia and Palm courses. Among them we find a familiar shape (bottom left). After a challenging game of golf, guests can relax in The Disney Inn's 60-foot pool, or bask in the Florida sunshine at poolside.

Discovery Island

Discovery Island is a tropical haven for rare and endangered species from all over the world. Here we find a rainbow of birds and wild animals.

Some of the 500 creatures that make their homes on Discovery Island are classified as endangered or threatened, like the toco toucan and the white crested hornbill. Others, like the bald eagle and the brown pelican, have been injured, and can no longer survive in the wild.

Discovery Island inhabitants are given as many opportunities as possible to roam free. As we wind through the shadowed pathways, it is difficult to realize that we are walking through enclosed spaces.

Discovery Island's conservation efforts were officially recognized in 1981, when the island was made an accredited zoological park by the American Association of Zoological Parks and Aquariums.

During Discovery Island's first six years, it was called "Treasure Island," after the Disney motion picture based on Robert Louis Stevenson's pirate novel. The abandoned wreck of the sailing ship Hispaniola *(top) still reclines on the beach today. The island itself (bottom left) was just a scruffy patch of green until Disney imagineers transformed it into a tropical paradise.*

While exploring Discovery Island, we may encounter a cuddly hyacinth macaw (top left), a toco toucan (center left), a marmoset (center), rose cockatoos (center right), a palm cockatoo and some more macaws (above left), an Indian white-crested hornbill (above center), a flock of colorful flamingoes (above right), a Galapagos tortoise (right) or an albino peacock (far right). The tortoise weighs in at about 300 pounds, and his species is endangered in its native habitat.

Disney's Fort Wilderness Resort and Campground

Ranging across nearly 650 acres, Disney's Fort Wilderness Resort and Campground blends the rustic charm of a frontier settlement with facilities and amenities appreciated by contemporary pioneers.

Stands of ancient cypress trees bearded with Spanish moss, huge pines and white-flowering bay trees border campsites that are from 25 to 65 feet long. Each campsite integrates beauty with privacy in this outdoor setting.

Campers can enjoy miles of winding trails on day or evening nature hikes, or take to forest pathways set aside for jogging or bicycling.

Nightly campfire gatherings at Fort Wilderness offer screenings of Disney cartoons and sing-alongs with a western guitarist.

Trail rides are available at the Tri-Circle-D Ranch. Not far away is a farm where children can pet ponies, sheep, rabbits, pygmy goats and other friendly critters.

Fort Wilderness proved so popular after Walt Disney World's opening that the number of campsites was doubled in 1972. This rustic campground's popularity shows no sign of waning, and expansion continues today. Campers hearing the call of the wild may take a horseback ride, paddle a canoe, or enjoy a nature walk.

At the Tri-Circle-D Ranch (above), we can watch a blacksmith practice his ancient art. Pioneer Hall (below) was designed to resemble a lodge in the Northwest Territory at the turn of the 19th century. It was constructed with 1,283 hand-fitted logs shipped by rail from Montana. The Pioneer Hall players (top right) serve up the wildest show in the West, the Hoop-Dee-Doo Revue.

River Country

For a splashin' good time, 1800s style, come to River Country. This Disney version of an old-fashioned swimmin' hole features the Upstream Plunge, Slippery Slide Falls, Whoop 'n' Holler Hollow, Raft Rider Ridge and White Water Rapids.

Disney engineers called upon gravity to keep River Country's million gallons of water fresh in its sheltered cove. A giant flexible tube at the mouth of the Ol' Swimmin' Hole, which opens into Bay Lake, expands and contracts to keep the River Country water level six inches higher than the lake. Lake water is pumped to the top of two giant flumes and a raft ride at the rate of 8,500 gallons a minute. Since gravity causes water to seek its own level, the River Country water spills over the top of the tube back into Bay Lake, providing needed circulation.

Disney's Village Resort

Disney's Village Resort offers an assortment of recreational activities, shopping and dining experiences, guest services and lodging, all blended into a wooded 4,000-acre corner of the Vacation Kingdom.

The community's Hotel Plaza has seven major independently owned and operated hotels, each offering various recreational activities.

Disney's Village Resort also offers unique villas in a variety of settings. They are more than merely attractive and spacious; they are proof that beautiful and efficient housing can harmonize with the environment.

The Vacation Villas, the Treehouse Villas, the Club Suites and the Fairway Villas all were designed to showcase energy-efficient housing ideas. And to conserve as much space as possible for parks and recreation, all the Villas are clustered around courtyards and cul-de-sacs, instead of built in a grid pattern.

Disney Village Marketplace

Disney's Village Resort also features swimming, tennis, and a par-72 golf course, complete with pro shop. Designed with mid-handicap players in mind, the Lake Buena Vista Golf Course is nonetheless challenging enough for a professional. At the heart of the resort community is a treasury of charming waterfront shops, boutiques, and restaurants known as Disney Village Marketplace. In place of the usual shopping-center chrome and steel architecture are weathered bricks, rich woods, and cedar shingles, to promote an atmosphere of warmth and intimacy. Extensively landscaped and embracing the 35-acre Lake Buena Vista, the Disney Village Marketplace reflects the same keen sense of design continuity found throughout the Vacation Kingdom. But while the Marketplace is harmonious, it is hardly homogenized. Each shop is stocked with its own pleasant surprises, and every restaurant and lounge is flavored with distinctive design accents. Like the Magic Kingdom and EPCOT Center, the Disney Village Marketplace is a walker's paradise. Numerous shaded benches and outdoor cafes encourage guests to slow down, relax, and enjoy the peaceful atmosphere.

Within the charming confines of Disney's Village Resort are excellent dining, shopping, and entertainment. You can enjoy a view of the Village Lake from Chef Mickey's Restaurant (top), browse at the many boutique-like shops, or watch one of the many seasonal outdoor entertainments.

Disney's Caribbean Beach Resort

Offering all the tranquil charm of an island paradise for a moderate cost, Disney's Caribbean Beach Resort rises at the edge of Barefoot Bay, a 42-acre lake, just moments from EPCOT.

Individual villages themed to reflect the color and style of Caribbean islands make up the large, comfortable resort. At its hub is Old Port Royale with cool stone walls, pirate cannons, exotic birds and flowers creating an inviting atmosphere for shopping, dining or taking a dip in the "ancient" Spanish fort that serves as a framework for a meandering pool.

Guests can cycle or walk along a picturesque promenade linking the villages. A footbridge leads to Parrot Cay Island, a play area where children can romp while adults enjoy the sunset.

Typhoon Lagoon

The surf's always up at Typhoon Lagoon, a water-play paradise created (according to Disney Legend) by the converging forces of a typhoon, earthquake and tidal wave. The result was a 56-acre water theme park that includes the world's largest man-made watershed mountain, Mount Mayday. Topped by a stranded shrimp boat, the Miss Tillie, it is the home of twisting, turning water slides including the Humunga Kowabunga (whose name says it all)!

The state-of-the-art water adventure also includes Shark Reef, a salt-water tank stocked with denizens of the deep for guests to observe as they snorkel or walk through a sunken tanker with viewing windows. Small fry can get even wetter behind the ears in Ketchakiddie Creek, a children's area equipped with marvelous water toys. Daring souls can catch man-made waves in a surfing pool, and those with a yen for travel can inner tube through misty rain forests on Castaway Creek.

With its colorful past, Typhoon Lagoon offers families innovative recreation that is sure to become legendary in its own time!

Pleasure Island

Pleasure Island provides a different dimension in entertainment at the Walt Disney World Resort.

Located across from the Disney Village Marketplace, the good-time getaway is designed to create the illusion of an historic waterfront restoration. It is inspired by the antics and achievements of its legendary proprietor Merriweather Adam Pleasure, whose fun-loving spirit is manifested in every inch of what was once supposedly his domain.

Buildings constructed to look as if they are part of a renovated waterfront district house themed nightclubs like the Mannequins Dance Palace, where guests mingle with animated and live mannequins on a rotating dance floor, or the Neon Armadillo Music Saloon which features country music in a southwestern setting. The Comedy Warehouse serves up refreshing laughs, and guests can get with the beat at the three-floor XZFR Rock & Roll Beach Club. Restaurants and snack facilities, as well as innovative shops displaying a variety of stylish merchandise, are clustered along Pleasure Island's byways.

From off-the-wall comedy to high-energy workouts on the dance floor, Pleasure Island serves up plenty of kinetic entertainment for energetic adults of all ages. Each evening of merriment is capped off with a wild celebration of New Year's Eve—complete with fireworks.

Walt Disney once said...

"The inclination of my life – the motto, you might call it – has been to do things and make things which will give pleasure to people in new and amusing ways. By doing that I please and satisfy myself. It is my wish to delight all members of the family, young and old, parent and child."

WO127-10003/1190